LITTLE BOOK OF

WELSH RUGBY

PLAYER BY PLAYER

Liam McCann

LITTLE BOOK OF

WELSH RUGBY

PLAYER BY PLAYER

First published in the UK in 2015

www.demand-media.co.uk

Printed and bound in Europe

ISBN 978-1-910540-45-9

Contents

Foreword
by John Dawes

To play for Wales was very special. As a youngster, you could only hope to play for your country in your wildest dreams but you don't really expect it to happen. So to have the privilege and honour of playing, captaining and coaching Wales during a magical time for Welsh rugby was way beyond my expectations.

As a humble valley boy from Abercarn, I didn't have the normal background for becoming skipper. People who played for Cardiff, Swansea, Newport and Llanelli were usually appointed.

I made my Wales debut against Ireland in 1964 at Lansdowne Road in Dublin and we managed to win 15-8. To be able to play alongside outside-half greats like David Watkins and Barry John was an amazing experience. To me, they typified the natural flair that was synonymous with Welsh rugby. My vision had always been for Wales to play with the efficiency of the New Zealand All Blacks, the power of South Africa and the flair of the French but, if I could only choose one component, it would be flair.

Welsh players seem to have it in abundance. It's something you can't teach so I think we must have been blessed with the gift. Max Boyce's outside-half factory might have been mythical but his song best epitomised Welsh rugby. For years, number 10s kept pouring off that imaginary conveyor belt. We saw, during the 2008 Grand Slam, the latest in James Hook and there are many more on the way. In my lifetime, we have had Cliff Morgan, David Watkins, Barry John, Phil Bennett and Jonathan Davies, all players with the ability to produce a flash of brilliance to change the course of a match.

More people play soccer than rugby in Wales but we are best at the oval ball game. Union has always been a classless sport that has united the population. Professionals like solicitors and accountants joined forces with miners and steelworkers. As soon as they walked into the dressing room at their club or with the national team, they became one. The camaraderie and commitment has always shone through. The competition between villages, the tribalism and the passion has always been intense but bring it together in the red jersey and the collective force has been far greater than the sum of its parts. This is what other countries respect about Welsh ruby, particularly the All Blacks.

During my tenure as captain and coach, I was fortunate to be surrounded by some marvellously talented players and we enjoyed great success. I had the privilege of being captain of the British & Irish Lions in New Zealand in 1971. And it was the Welsh players who provided the bedrock for that historic series triumph and the unbeaten tour of South Africa three years later.

I could reel off the names of backs who have starred for Wales but we've also produced some of the game's greatest forwards: Rhys Williams, Bryn Meredith, Russell Robins and Clem Thomas spring to mind but there are so many more.

Unfortunately, Wales lost many big names to rugby league and a fair proportion became household names in the 13-a-side game. If they hadn't gone north, we might well have had more success on the domestic front and in the international arena. The threat from league has virtually disappeared since union went professional in 1995, however, and we now have another fine crop of players like George North, Leigh Halfpenny and Jamie Roberts establishing themselves in the Test arena. Grand Slams are not to be sniffed at and this generation managed it in 2005, 2008 and 2012. It's fantastic. For too long, the country has been living in the past and dwelling on the achievements of Edwards and John in the 1960s and 1970s, but it's time to move on and celebrate the players of today.

The current stars appear in this book alongside the greats of yesteryear. Try picking a best Welsh XV from those listed here. It's not easy!

Introduction

The game that was played on the fields of Rugby School throughout the 18th and 19th centuries was codified by three sixth-form pupils in 1845 (so there were no set laws about running with the ball in hand when William Webb Ellis supposedly broke the rules in 1823). By 1863, the amateur clubs that had been founded by public-school leavers formed the Football Association, although Blackheath immediately left the organisation in a dispute over the rules relating to hacking opponents' legs. One faction developed into the FA of today, while the other, which favoured handling the ball, became the Rugby Football Union in 1871.

RIGHT The Welsh rugby team before their 1895 clash against England

The 1870s saw the game spread around the world, first to Australia and New Zealand and then to Canada, the United States and South Africa. In the USA, the scrum was replaced with the line of scrimmage and forward passes were allowed, while in Ireland, football and rugby merged to form Gaelic Football.

The Home Nations Championship between England, Ireland, Scotland and Wales was introduced in 1883. Five years later, a representative side from the UK, which would eventually become the British & Irish Lions, toured New Zealand and Australia but, when the party returned to England, the RFU held an investigation into illegal payments to players. Jack Clowes had been reimbursed for his travel expenses so he was banned by the RFU. (This foreshadowed the 1895 split between the league and union codes, with the latter remaining amateur until 1995.)

Over the next 70 years, the sport

Linesman. Jackson. F. Mills. T. W. Pearson. A. W. Boucher. W. Elsey. Selwyn Biggs.

C. B. Nicholl. J. Hannen. C. Badger. W. H. Watts. A. J. Gould. W. J. Bancroft. T. C. Graham. Davies. L. Thomas.

WALES.

ABOVE The immortals who beat New Zealand in 1905

reached all corners of the globe. Although games between the home unions and the colonies were initially one-sided, New Zealand and South Africa adopted rugby as their national sport and it was seen as a rite of passage to play at school. The southern hemisphere teams are now the dominant forces, but there's no doubt they based their electrifying brand of rugby on one team: Wales in the 1970s.

The first golden era for Welsh rugby had come at the turn of the century, however. The side had a tough baptism on the international stage when they were trounced by England in 1881, but by the mid-1890s they'd revolutionised the game by adopting a new formation comprising seven backs and eight forwards. They won a Triple Crown in 1893 and took another championship win in 1900. Two more titles followed in 1902 and 1905.

In 1905, the mighty All Blacks came to Cardiff Arms Park. It was a game that pitched a Welsh side unbeaten at home in six years against a touring outfit that was unbeaten in all their provincial matches as well as Tests against England, Ireland and Scotland. New Zealand performed their haka challenge and the Welsh crowd responded with *Land of Our Fathers,* the first time the national anthem had been sung before a sporting event. Welsh winger Teddy Morgan scored

The great Teddy Morgan in 1905

the decisive try and condemned the All Blacks to their only defeat on the 35-match tour.

The 1908 England versus Wales game at Bristol was so affected by fog that the Welsh didn't realise they'd left fullback Bert Winfield on the pitch at the end. They were all relaxing in the clubhouse celebrating a 28-19 win by the time someone realised he was missing. Apparently Winfield believed his side had been camped on the England line for the entire second half.

Wales dominated the 1906, 1909 and 1910 championships, the latter being the first official Five Nations as the French had been invited to join the tournament. The following year, Wales won a Grand Slam after victories over each of their four rivals. It would be their last Grand Slam for four decades, however, as England became the dominant force immediately before the First World War.

The post-war years were equally grim in Wales: a recession led to many players defecting to the professional code and the side only won seven matches in a six-year period in the mid-1920s (five of which were against France). The 1930s brought renewed hope and Wales secured a championship win in 1931. They went on to beat the All Blacks in 1935 but the Second World War saw the Five Nations cancelled until 1947.

This was the world's premier tournament in the 1950s. There was no southern hemisphere equivalent so, although the All Blacks and the other nations sent touring sides abroad, they rarely played in a championship format. Towards the end of the decade, Australian player Harold Tolhurst submitted an idea for a World Cup but the International Rugby Board refused to sanction it.

Wales won their first Grand Slam after the war in 1950. They backed it up with another two years later and then beat the touring All Blacks. Conditions were so bad during the 1957 Wales-Ireland clash in Cardiff that referee Jack Taylor ordered the entire Welsh team from the field after an hour because their shirts were so black with mud. The clean kit worked wonders and the Welsh went on to win.

Welsh fullback Terry Davies was denied a winning penalty by the goalpost at Twickenham in 1958. Later that night, Welsh jockey Fred Mathias and Englishman Brian Attewell broke into the ground and, having failed to remove the offending post, sawed off the crossbar and took it back to Pembrokeshire. They bumped into Davies on the way home and he autographed the bar, then, as the RFU had intervened, and he was a timber merchant, he agreed to replace the crossbar instead of having the original returned.

The side endured a slump in form between 1957 and 1963 but, despite regaining the title in 1964, they were then thumped by South Africa (24-3) on their first overseas tour. It was this defeat that proved the catalyst for change and brought about a revolution in coaching and attitude.

The WRU appointed David Nash as the national coach but he was soon replaced by Clive Rowlands. The team he built is as revered as the Brazilian football side of the same era. The likes of JPR and JJ Williams, Gareth Edwards, John Dawes, Barry John and Gerald and Mervyn Davies transformed the game into a living

LEFT Willie Llewellyn captained Wales during their first golden era

work of art. The side lost only a handful of Five Nations matches in a decade and ushered in the second golden age of Welsh rugby. The principality contributed the majority of players for the Lions tour to New Zealand in 1971 and they won the series 2-1. Much of the same side then defeated South Africa on the legendary 1974 tour.

The Welsh dominated the Five Nations for the remainder of the decade but Australia and New Zealand still refused to be silenced on the subject of a World Cup. They had already submitted separate bids, which had been turned down by the IRB, so they then joined forces and resubmitted a more comprehensive bid to co-host the first tournament. They suggested staging it in 1987 so it didn't clash with the Olympic Games or the FIFA World Cup and presented their feasibility study to the IRB in 1985. When France threw their weight behind a tournament in the southern hemisphere (on the condition that countries not affiliated to the IRB would also be invited), the IRB was forced into a corner and had to take a vote. South Africa voted in favour, even though they would be excluded from any tournament due to apartheid, and this prompted England and Wales to follow suit. Only Ireland and Scotland voted against the tournament as they felt it threatened the game's amateur status. The IRB went with the vote and New Zealand and Australia hosted the event in 1987.

The Welsh weren't expected to do well. The side had been in decline for a decade and had only won 15 of 32 Five Nations matches since 1980. They progressed comfortably through their group, however, and it wasn't until the knockout phase of the tournament that the matches became competitive. The seven members of the IRB and Fiji reached the quarter-finals so there were no surprises in the pool stages. New Zealand were a class apart and demolished Scotland; Australia saw off a spirited Ireland; France beat Fiji comfortably; and Wales turned England over in Brisbane.

The two best matches of the tournament were the epic semi-final between Australia and France in Sydney, which France won in the dying moments, and the third-place playoff between Australia and Wales

LEFT David Watkins was one of the great Welsh standoffs of the 1950s and '60s

in Rotorua, which Wales won by a single point (giving the side its best finish at the tournament to date). In the final, New Zealand were too good for France in every department and they secured the trophy with a 29-9 win at Auckland's Eden Park.

The home unions hosted the second World Cup in 1991 but Welsh rugby was still in disarray after the side had been whitewashed in the 1990 Five Nations. Pool 3 delivered perhaps the greatest upset in the tournament's history when Western Samoa beat Wales 16-13 in Cardiff. This left the Welsh needing to beat favourites Australia in their final group match, but they were eliminated from the tournament after a 38-3 drubbing.

Four years later, Wales again failed to qualify from their group at the World Cup in South Africa after a one-point loss to Ireland in their final pool game. By Graham Henry's appointment as head coach in 1998, however, the Welsh were showing signs of a resurgence and he led them on a 10-match winning streak that included victory over the world champion South Africans. It proved to be a false dawn, however. In 1999,

OPPOSITE Wales went on to finish third in the 1987 World Cup after beating England

LEFT Kevin Mosley wins the ball from John Eales during the 1991 World Cup

ABOVE Neil Jenkins kicks for goal during the match against Argentina played at his beloved Millennium Stadium in 1999

Wales lost again to Samoa (38-31) in a thrilling World Cup match at the new Millennium Stadium in Cardiff. Although they beat Argentina and Japan, they lost convincingly to Australia in the quarter-final. Henry then resigned after poor showings in the 2001 and 2002 Six Nations. Under his co-manager, Steve Hansen, Wales at last showed signs of recovery at the 2003 World Cup in Australia: they thrashed Canada, then squeezed past Tonga and Italy before facing co-favourites the All Blacks in front of 80,000 in Sydney.

New Zealand's performances in the group stage had included thumping wins over Italy, Canada and Tonga and they were also expected to see off Wales, but no one could have foreseen such a pulsating encounter.

The All Blacks started quickly and Joe Rokocoko immediately scored in the corner. Leon MacDonald added the conversion and the Welsh were 7-0 down before they'd touched the ball. The All Blacks continued pouring forwards but the Welsh defence held firm and Mark Taylor scored after a scintillating counterattack. Stephen Jones added the conversion and the sides were level.

Barely a minute later, Rokocoko raced down the left wing and cut inside the Welsh defence for his second try.

MacDonald added the conversion but Wales almost scored direct from the restart. Jones kicked a penalty instead and the deficit was cut to four.

Justin Marshall, Richie McCaw and Jerry Collins then combined in the midfield to give New Zealand a great position. When the Welsh gave away a penalty, Marshall slipped the ball to MacDonald and he went over for a third All Black try. He then added the conversion to give the Kiwis an 11-point lead. The All Blacks stretched their lead when Ali Williams collected Carlos Spencer's cross-field kick to score in the corner. MacDonald added the extras and the early Welsh promise was a distant memory.

Shane Williams then sold the Kiwis a dummy and burst through the defence before delivering the crucial pass for Sonny Parker to score. Jones added another difficult conversion and then Colin Charvis dived over from close range for yet another international try. Jones kicked the conversion to bring the Welsh within four at the break.

He added a penalty immediately after halftime, and then Wales took the lead after Sweeney and Charvis broke up the middle before releasing Shane Williams. Ever dependable with the boot, Jones added the conversion and Wales were suddenly six points clear. The All Blacks replied immediately with a Doug Howlett try but MacDonald couldn't convert and Jones added another penalty for Wales. New Zealand saw first Mils Muliaina and then Kees Meeuws held up over the line but the Welsh defence was eventually breached when Carlos Spencer slipped over off the back of a scrum. Marshall then released Howlett for his second of the match but MacDonald couldn't add the conversion and Wales were still in the game with 10 minutes to go.

MacDonald put the All Blacks nine points clear with a late penalty, and an Aaron Mauger try finally sealed a fabulous win in which Wales had played the majority of the rugby. The All Blacks were expected to go on and win the tournament but hosts Australia beat them in the semi-final. The defeat meant the Welsh faced England in the knockout phase.

The tournament co-favourites had marched through their group with only one brief scare against Samoa and they started the quarter-final brightly when Matt Dawson broke up-field. Jonny Wilkinson only hit the post with a penalty for offside, however. The Welsh then launched a flowing backline move but Robert Sidoli knocked the ball on over the English line.

It took until the 18th minute before Wilkinson finally notched a penalty for England, and the men in white then pounded the Welsh line for 10 phases. Wales held out, turned the ball over and counterattacked: Shane Williams collected a cross-field kick meant for Ben Kay. He sidestepped the second row and released the backs against scattered English defenders. He then juggled a difficult return pass before passing to Stephen Jones to score the try of the tournament. Wales turned down an easy penalty moments later and sent Colin Charvis over for a second try in five minutes.

Wales came out after the break and continued to play an expansive game with aggressive defence, but a long kick into England territory fell to Cohen who passed to Jason Robinson. The fullback tore through the Welsh cover, leaving five players in his wake before feeding Will Greenwood to score in the corner. Wilkinson converted from the touchline and the sides were level again. He then added five penalties in quick succession and the win seemed a formality, but Wales raised their game and Martyn Williams touched down after the English defence fumbled a cross-field kick. Iestyn Harris kicked the conversion and Wales were back in the contest. Harris had the chance to cut the lead in the 74th minute but he sliced a penalty and Wilkinson wrapped the game up with a last-minute drop-goal.

These performances, albeit in losing causes, dragged Welsh rugby out of the wilderness and they finally secured a ninth Grand Slam in 2005. Their 32-20 victory on the last day of the championship ended 27 years of heartache and disappointment, but the side had been improving steadily since the 2004 autumn internationals when they almost beat South Africa and the All Blacks. So hopes were high coming into the 2005 Six Nations but the big test came on February 5th against England.

Wales hadn't beaten England in Cardiff for 12 years and they came out with an intensity and purpose not seen in a generation. They may have dominated the match but they hadn't converted all their chances into scores and England fought back from a converted Shane Williams try to hold a two-point lead in the dying minutes. When England captain Jason Robinson was penalised for not releasing the ball in the ruck, Gavin Henson stepped up and knocked over

BELOW Colin Charvis holds the world record for the most number of tries by a forward (22)

the penalty from 45 metres to seal the victory. Shane Williams almost added a second try with the last touch of the game but it didn't matter as the Welsh won 11-9.

Wales had faltered against the Italians in Rome in 2003 and the memories were still fresh, but the Welsh were determined to exorcise the ghost with breathtaking attacking rugby. Williams was at his brilliant best on the wing and he tormented the Azzurri throughout the match with his jinking runs. Brent Cockbain scored on debut, Martyn Williams added a second when he touched down at the base of the post, and Robert Sidoli bagged a third against his homeland. The final score of 38-8 to Wales probably flattered the Italians and the Welsh headed to Paris in buoyant mood.

Their initial confidence looked to be misplaced as the French started aggressively and played with the carefree abandon and Gallic flair so often associated with the side. Mike Ruddock's men found themselves 15-6 down at halftime at the Stade de France so something special was needed to lift the men in red. Martyn Williams provided the catalyst with two remarkable tries but there were nervous moments as Gareth Thomas went off with a broken thumb and Stephen Jones momentarily misfired with the boot. The Welsh eventually extended their lead to six, however, and clung on to the end in the face of waves of French attacks. With three wins out of three, people began to dream about an elusive Grand Slam.

Having fought back so well in Paris, Murrayfield suddenly didn't seem so intimidating. Wales continued where they'd left off and played an expansive attacking game. Ryan Jones started a move deep within his own half and it was he who provided the touchdown at the other end after a breathless counterattack. Wales were suddenly rampant and they opened up a 38-3 lead before the Scots knew what had hit them. Three tries in the opening 15 minutes had practically finished them off, although they did rally and eventually scored 22 points. The game had long since ceased to be a contest, however, and Wales won by 24 points. Now all thoughts turned to Ireland in Cardiff, the biggest game on Welsh soil since the World Cup in 1999.

It could have been a Grand Slam decider had Ireland not been beaten by France but the championship was still up for grabs. Ireland hadn't lost in Cardiff for more than 20 years so the Welsh had the weight of the nation on their shoulders, but they were extremely fired up and had the scoreboard ticking over immediately when Gethin Jenkins charged down a clearance kick to score. The Welsh backs then treated the crowd to another exhibition of running rugby and Kevin Morgan eventually finished the move. Ireland tried to muscle their way back into the game but they were pinned back by Henson and Jones and Wales had the Grand Slam sewn up with a 12-point victory. Martyn Williams was pronounced man of the tournament despite not being expected to play because of injury.

After such a superb year, it came as something of a surprise when Wales were beaten by Italy in the 2006 Six Nations and only just avoided the wooden spoon. They were then drawn alongside Canada, Japan, Australia and Fiji at the 2007 World Cup. They beat Canada convincingly but lost to Australia by 12 points in Cardiff. They then thumped Japan but still had to win their final pool game against a Fijian side that played an exciting brand of rugby. What followed was perhaps the greatest game ever played.

The Welsh started fast and Shane Williams almost scored in the second minute after a length-of-the-field move. After 15 minutes, the Fijian pack rumbled up-field and Nicky Little converted Akapusi Qera's try under the posts. Fiji ran the ball from the restart and Vilimoni Delasau collected his own chip to score a magnificent solo effort. Although Little couldn't add the conversion, he then kicked a penalty to give Fiji a 15-3 lead. He added another two minutes later and Fiji scored a superb third try through Kele Leawere. Fiji were almost out of sight after only a quarter of the game.

The Welsh responded by hammering the Fijian defence. Alix Popham touched down after a scrum and James Hook added the conversion but Fiji maintained a 15-point lead at halftime. Shane Williams then scored a magnificent solo try, sidestepping three defenders and racing in from 80

metres. Hook added the conversion and the Welsh were within eight. Another superb backline move saw Gareth Thomas score on his 100th cap. Jones struck the post with the conversion so Fiji retained a three-point lead. A slick lineout move then saw Mark Jones scoring a super try in the opposite corner, and the Welsh appeared to have completed a miraculous comeback when Jones added the extras.

Little pegged the Welsh back with a penalty and then restored the Fijian lead with another after an hour. The game turned again when Martyn Williams intercepted a pass with seven minutes to go and ran 60 metres to score. Stephen Jones hit the post for the third time with the conversion. With only four minutes left, Graham Dewes scored from close range and Little added the conversion to give Fiji a four-point lead. It was a lead they maintained in the face of unrelenting Welsh pressure.

The defeat saw Gareth Jenkins replaced as head coach by Warren Gatland and the New Zealander masterminded a memorable win over England in his first match. Their excellent form continued throughout the 2008 Six Nations and Wales sealed a 10th Grand Slam with a 29-12 win over France on the last weekend.

Almost 100 years to the day had passed since the memorable 1908 Grand Slam and Wales also equalled France's two Grand Slams since the start of the Six Nations Championship. Gatland had drafted in Rob Howley and Shaun Edwards to the backroom staff and promoted Ryan Jones to the captaincy before the tournament. Edwards brought defensive nous and Howley was also tactically astute. The main aim was to get the ball to Shane Williams and let the diminutive winger cause havoc out wide.

England always provided a stern test at Twickenham and they were coming off the back of a World Cup final appearance, but Wales still had their epic 1999 Wembley triumph fresh in the memory. England made the brighter start, however, and they were 19-6 up at the break after Jonny Wilkinson had slotted three kicks, including the conversion for Toby Flood's try. Wales only had a couple of James Hook penalties to show for their efforts.

Wales couldn't impose themselves through the pack and England's front five dominated at the breakdown and set piece. Wilkinson's tactical kicking also had the Welsh turning and finding themselves on the defensive. Wales finally span the ball wide to Williams but the English defence was well organised and they kept him out. Hook cut the gap to 10 with a long-range penalty after Andrew Sheridan infringed at the lineout but Paul Sackey would have restored England's lead had Huw Bennett not saved a certain try. When Wilkinson kicked his third penalty just after the break, Wales looked beaten but Hook kept the visitors in touch with his third kick and Wales suddenly came to life when Henson burst past Wilkinson to set up a penalty chance on the hour. Hook knocked it over and England suddenly looked nervous as the Welsh closed to within seven points.

Wales scored a crucial try five minutes later when Hook beat three defenders to release Byrne in the corner. He then added the conversion to tie the scores. When Mike Phillips charged down Iain Balshaw's kick a few minutes later, Gethin Jenkins fed Shane Williams and the winger

LEFT Michael Owen takes a lineout against England

passed back inside for Phillips to beat Balshaw. Hook added a difficult conversion from the touchline and Wales recorded their first win at HQ since 1988.

With the ghosts of Twickenham laid to rest, Wales hosted Scotland in Cardiff the following week. Chris Paterson had kicked the Scots to victory the previous year so Gatland gave a start to Jamie Roberts and brought Tom Shanklin in for Sonny Parker at centre. Scotland also had a forward pack that could starve the Welsh of ball and give Paterson the platform to kick his goals so Wales never felt in command of the game. Indeed it was Paterson who opened the scoring on 10 minutes with a penalty. Wales tried to respond immediately as Duncan Jones, Ian Evans and Mike Phillips all went close but Scotland held firm.

The difference, as was so often the case, was Shane Williams. He scored his 36th Test try in the 13th minute after a sweeping move along the three-quarters. Three minutes later, Scotland lock Nathan Hines was sin-binned for a swinging arm but Wales couldn't make their man advantage count.

Hook landed a penalty on 28 minutes to increase the lead to seven points and Scotland suffered another blow when skipper Jason White had to go off injured after half an hour. Paterson kept the Scottish side of the scoreboard ticking over with the boot but Wales led 10-6 at the break. The stand-off reduced the lead to one with his third penalty just after the restart but this finally stung the Welsh into action and Hook scored a try two minutes later when Duncan Jones's pass opened up the Scottish defence.

Paterson kept Scotland in the game with his fourth and fifth penalties and at 17-15 they started to believe. Gatland responded by introducing the Llanelli Scarlets trio of Stephen Jones, Dwayne Peel and Matthew Rees and the substitutions proved inspired as Jones kicked Wales five points clear. Shane Williams then clinched the match with a brilliant solo try in which he left four Scottish defenders clutching midair and then held off the challenge of Nikki Walker in the corner. Although it seemed as if his foot had grazed the touchline, Italian TMO (television match official) Carlo Damasco awarded the try. Jones added the conversion and another penalty late on to secure an emphatic 30-15 victory. With his brace of tries, Williams became Wales's leading scorer in the Six Nations Championship.

Williams scored another two tries as Wales demolished Italy 47-8 at

LEFT Wales have produced some of the game's greatest number 10s. Here Stephen Jones kicks for the corner against England in 2006

the Millennium Stadium in the third round of the championship. The visitors made Wales work hard in the first half but Stephen Jones settled the nerves with an early penalty. They upped their game in the second period and ran in four unanswered tries. Jones had one of those perfect days when every kick was successful and he left the field to a standing ovation after bagging 18 points.

Gatland again used Mike Phillips as a super sub and he cut the Italian defence apart with his first touch and almost went the length of the field. Williams had been outstanding on the wing and he scored a brilliant second try that sealed the match and will be spoken of in hushed tones for generations. The win saw Gatland's side go top of the table with two games to play but Ireland still had aspirations of a Triple Crown and they had home advantage at Croke Park in Dublin.

Ireland had only just beaten Italy before losing to France in a tight match in Paris, although they'd then roared back to form with a big win over Scotland. This was Wales's first visit to the temporary home of Irish rugby but they arrived with the mindset that they would record their first win in Dublin since the turn of the millennium.

The home side drew first blood in the fourth minute when Ronan O'Gara landed a penalty, and he added a second after a quarter of the match. Stephen Jones pulled three points back but the hosts led 6-3 at the interval. It had been a lacklustre half in which Wales had played most of the rugby, although it needed some superb defensive work from the reliable Martyn Williams and skipper Ryan Jones to weather the early Irish storm. Wales gradually grew into the match but they didn't cross the whitewash until early in the second half when the magician Shane Williams held off two Irish defenders to score in the corner. The try brought him level with Gareth Thomas's Welsh record of 40 and extended his Six Nations record. Stephen Jones had been having a more difficult afternoon with the boot but he slotted the difficult conversion to give Wales a 13-6 lead.

O'Gara reduced the deficit to a single point with two penalties after Martyn Williams had been sent to the bin for a professional foul, but Wales didn't panic and James Hook sealed a narrow win with a penalty four minutes from time. Wales only needed to beat France in Cardiff to secure a second Grand Slam in four seasons, but the French could still take the championship with a win. The expectation was palpable, the tension unbearable.

Marc Lievremont named the strongest possible French side but no one was predicting they could turn the Welsh over by the 20 points they needed to win the title. Gatland stuck with his big guns as the rain began to fall in South Wales. Both sides agreed to close the stadium roof and lock Ian Gough led the team out on the occasion of his 50th cap.

Wales seemed to be feeling the pressure in the first few minutes as hooker Huw Bennett missed his first lineout and Lee Byrne saw a drop goal fall short. James Hook finally settled the nerves in the fifth minute with a moment of magic when his delightful short pass released Tom Shanklin. He slipped the ball to Mark Jones but the wing stumbled with the line at his mercy.

Hook opened the scoring with a penalty from the resulting scrum and the French then lost their way with some awful kicking. Hook added a second penalty before Jean-Baptiste Elissalde reduced the deficit to three with a kick of his own. Hook restored Wales's six-point lead after quarter of the match and Wales then withstood a brief French resurgence. Elissalde eventually cut the deficit to three when Gavin Henson was given a yellow card for a high tackle on Fulgence Ouedraogo just before the break.

Elissalde drew the French level with his third penalty early in the second half but Wales held out and Henson's return shored up the midfield. Yannick Jauzion then dropped the ball on the hour and Shane Williams pounced. He hacked it over the line and dived on it to score the try that broke Gareth Thomas's record. Stephen Jones had come on for Hook so he converted the score and Wales were suddenly in control.

Jones added a penalty on the hour to extend their lead to 10 but Dimitri Yachvili reduced the deficit to seven with a penalty 11 minutes from time. Jones replied again for the Welsh before Martyn Williams burst through the tiring French cover with four minutes on the clock. It was perhaps fitting that the two best players in the

tournament sealed the win and gave Wales their 10th Grand Slam.

The 2009 campaign wasn't as successful and Wales surrendered the title to Ireland, but Gatland's attacking philosophy was paying dividends and they entered the 2011 World Cup in confident mood. A one-point defeat to South Africa was followed by solid wins over Samoa, Namibia and Fiji so they qualified comfortably for the knockout phase.

The quarter-finals were low-scoring affairs with only New Zealand progressing easily after a 33-10 win over Argentina. A resurgent Wales finally lived up to expectation with a 22-10 victory against Ireland. The first semi-final was another tight encounter that Wales should have won but captain Sam Warburton was harshly sent off after 18 minutes and James Hook missed two crucial penalties to allow France to scrape through by a point. New Zealand lived up to their favourites tag by beating Australia in the second semi but they almost choked in the final. The French had broken their hearts twice before but this time the All Blacks held on to win their first title in 24 years. Wales played their part in an entertaining bronze-medal match against Australia but the Wallabies won 21-18.

The Welsh carried their form into the 2012 Six Nations and secured their third Grand Slam in eight years, avenging the loss to France in the last game of the tournament. They kicked off the championship with a superb 23-21 victory over Ireland at the new Aviva Stadium but the hosts seemed to be in control when Bradley Davies was yellow carded and Tommy Bowe scored a try while he was in the bin.

George North replied for the visitors to bring Wales within a point but Ireland held this lead gong into the last minute. Stephen Ferris was then sin binned for a controversial spear tackle on Ian Evans and Leigh Halfpenny held his nerve to kick the penalty that gave the visitors a two-point win.

The second round of the championship saw Wales host Scotland at the Millennium Stadium. Greig Laidlaw may have scored all 13 points for the Scots but the Cardiff Blues combination of try-scorer Alex Cuthbert and kicking maestro Leigh Halfpenny – who also chipped in with a

LEFT Gareth Thomas has been one of the most influential Welsh captains

GRAND SLAM
RBS 6 NATIONS CHAMPIONS 2012
RBS NATIONS

brace of tries – gave Wales a 29-13 win.

Twickenham may have once been England's fortress but Scott Williams turned the game on its head five minutes from time with a brilliant solo try. Leigh Halfpenny and Owen Farrell had both kicked four penalties so the scores were tied at 12-12. Williams then stole the ball from Courtney Lawes and kicked ahead. He beat the exhausted defence to the ball and stunned Twickenham into silence as Wales collected a Triple Crown. They now only needed to beat Italy and France to deliver a third Grand Slam of the new millennium.

Italy were dispatched 24-3 in Cardiff and Wales raised their game once more to record an 11th clean sweep with a 16-9 win over France at the Millennium Stadium, Alex Cuthbert scoring the only try of the match. Having reached the highs, the Welsh then inexplicably endured a torrid run of eight consecutive defeats. They recovered in time for the 2013 Six Nations, however, and only lost to Ireland on their way to retaining the trophy for the first time in 35 years.

Wales could only edge past Italy in a disappointing opener to their 2014 campaign and they were then hammered by Ireland. The Welsh bounced back and thumped a lacklustre France before being outplayed by England at Twickenham. They finished the tournament on a high with a 48-point annihilation of Scotland and carried this form into the autumn international series against the southern hemisphere sides.

Despite losing narrowly to Australia and New Zealand, they beat Fiji and rounded off a solid season with victory over South Africa. The 2015 Six Nations saw Wales lose to England but they then beat Ireland, France and Scotland to leave themselves with a chance of the championship. Having demolished Italy in their last game, they held a slight points advantage over both England and Ireland. Both rivals won their matches convincingly, however, and Wales eventually finished third in the table despite only losing one match.

Wales have perhaps the toughest group at the 2015 World Cup. Australia, England and Fiji will provide stern tests as only Uruguay lack the depth and structure to compete at the highest level.

LEFT Another Welsh Grand Slam in 2012

Bassett

Bassett's rugby career began with Kenfig Hill and Pyle but, having joined the police, he played for the Constabulary and Penarth. In 1928, the national selectors were looking for a dependable fullback and Bassett was chosen to represent his country after a one-off game against Newport.

He earned his first international cap against England in an 8-3 defeat at Twickenham the following year, and by 1930 he'd been appointed captain of Wales. He enjoyed a great start to the 1930 Five Nations and single-handedly saved his side against Ireland. He would have taken the field against the French but he'd already been called up for the British Lions and was on his way to Australia. (Wales finished the domestic championship as runners up to England.)

He had an exceptional tour, outplaying local hero George Nepia in the tourists' four matches against New Zealand, and, having earned the nickname 'Rock of Gibraltar' for his heavy tackling, was immediately proclaimed the best fullback in world rugby. He played in five Test matches on the tour and his powerful defence often turned ball over for the Lions to use in attack. When he returned home, he guided Wales to their first Home Nations Championship in a decade.

He was criticised for his poor tactics against the touring South Africans in 1931 but he retained the captaincy and helped Wales win their first two matches in the 1932 Five Nations. Then the wheels fell off, however. He dropped a high ball and gifted Ireland a try, then missed a tackle to allow the Irish in for a second score. The Triple Crown could still have been sealed had Bassett kicked a last-minute conversion but he missed, ending his international career with a share of the championship.

RIGHT John Bassett, Wales Captain

....Having earned the nickname 'Rock of Gibraltar' for his heavy tackling, was immediately proclaimed the best fullback in world rugby.

Name: John Archibald 'Jack' Bassett
Born: 11th July 1905, Trebanog, Wales
Died: 19th February 1989, Cardiff
Position: Fullback
Height: 5'10" (1.78m)
Weight: 189lbs (86kg)
International Career: 1929 - 1932
International Caps: 20
International Points: 29
Honours: Five Nations Championship (1931)

Bebb

The son of Welsh historian Ambrose Bebb, Dewi was educated at Friars School and Trinity College, Carmarthen. The North Walian had been Welsh Schools senior 440-yard and long-jump champion, and he had also been capped at rugby by the Welsh Secondary Schools XV. He was a talented and pacey wing who made his first-team debut for Swansea against Llanelli in 1958. In all, he would make 221 appearances for the club, scoring 87 tries and captaining them for two seasons, 1963-65.

He won the first of his 34 caps for Wales against England in 1959. He scored the decisive try and was carried from the Arms Park pitch by ecstatic fans. Having proved himself a potent winger, he was selected for Wales's first overseas tour in 1964, although he'd already been abroad with the Lions in South Africa two years previously. The tourists won 16 of their 25 games but lost three of the four Tests.

He scored 11 tries for his country, including a trademark break from a lineout as Wales clinched a 10th Triple Crown by beating Ireland at Cardiff Arms Park in 1965. In 1966, Bebb was again asked to tour with the Lions. The Australian leg went to plan as the tourists won five of six provincial matches and hammered the hosts in both Tests. But the New Zealanders were a much tougher proposition and the Lions lost all three Tests against the All Blacks. They did manage to beat Canada in Toronto on the way home, however.

He retired from the game in 1967 and became a successful broadcaster and journalist.

RIGHT Dewi Bebb breaks a tackle from England's Simon Clarke

He won the first of his 34 caps for Wales against England in 1959. He scored the decisive try and was carried from the Arms Park pitch by ecstatic fans.

Name: Dewi Iorwerth Ellis Bebb
Born: 7th August 1938, Bangor, Wales
Died: 14th March 1996, Pontypridd
Position: Wing
Height: 5'9" (1.76m)
Weight: 158lbs (72kg)
International Career: 1959 - 1967
International Caps: 42
International Points: 36
Honours: Five Nations Championship (1964, 1965, 1966)

Bennett

Bennett had a superb sidestep, searing pace and dazzling skills that would see him become one of the best-loved players of his generation. At the age of just 20 he became the first substitute for Wales when he came on in Paris for the injured Gerald Davies. He occasionally played at centre or fullback but, when the great Barry John retired, he made the fly-half position his own.

Bennett's supreme skills were showcased at the legendary game between the Barbarians and the All Blacks in Cardiff in 1973, and it was he who sidestepped three opponents before launching the famous counterattack that saw Gareth Edwards score the best try in the game's history. (He'd previously masterminded Llanelli's epic win over the All Blacks.)

In what was fast-becoming a golden age for Welsh rugby, Bennett was a shoe-in for the 1974 Lions tour to South Africa and he didn't disappoint, scoring more than 100 points and obliterating the hosts' defence with a 50-yard solo run in Pretoria. The Lions would go on to win the match comfortably, 28-9. The tour was a resounding success and the Lions won 21 of 22 matches, with a solitary draw in the final Test, and they restricted the physically imposing South Africans to just 34 points in the four matches.

On the domestic front, competition for places meant that Bennett was dropped in 1975 but he returned to the national team the following year and took over as captain from Mervyn Davies. Wales flopped in front of a world-record crowd of 104,000 in Edinburgh, however, and he was lucky

RIGHT Phil Bennett makes an outside break for Wales

Name: Phil Bennett, OBE
Born: 24th October 1948, Felinfoel, Wales
Position: Fly-half
Height: 5'7" (1.71m)
Weight: 163lbs (74kg)
International Career: 1969 - 1978
International Caps: 37
International Points: 210
Honours: Five Nations Championship (1969, 1970, 1971, 1973, 1976, 1978), Five Nations Grand Slam (1971, 1976, 1978), Lions Series Winner (1971, 1974)

to retain his place. A fortnight later, he started against Ireland at Cardiff Arms Park and he masterminded a magnificent 32-4 demolition of the men in green. He was one of the stars of the Five Nations Grand Slam teams of 1976 and 1978, but his greatest game came when captaining Wales in the decider against France in Cardiff. On the Wednesday before the game, he had withdrawn with an injury but was persuaded to play with protection around his right foot and he scored two tries in an epic 16-7 win.

Welsh rugby was still the dominant force in Europe so he was also selected to captain the 1977 Lions on their tour to New Zealand. (His pre-match talk in the Five Nations encounter against England earlier in the year is the stuff of legend: "Look what these people have done to Wales. They've taken our coal, our water, our steel. They buy our homes and live in them for a fortnight every year. What have they given us? Absolutely nothing. We've been exploited, raped, controlled and punished by the English, and that's who you are playing this afternoon." Wales won 14-5.)

Consistent rain meant the pitches in New Zealand were heavy and stifled his expansive running game so he became isolated, homesick and disillusioned on a tour that several players wanted to forget. The Lions outplayed the All Blacks upfront but never quite got going out wide. They lost the first Test but won the second and were only denied a share of the series by a late try in the fourth that gave New Zealand a one-point victory. Despite his confidence problem, and the treatment he was receiving from the All Black back row, Bennett was the Lions' top scorer with 112 points.

Bennett had a superb sidestep, searing pace and dazzling skills.

Of their 26 matches, they won 21 and lost five, but they also lost a Test match in Fiji on the way home (25-21), although they did beat the Barbarians at Twickenham as part of the queen's silver jubilee celebrations.

He retired in 1978, was inducted into the International Rugby Hall of Fame in 2005 and the Welsh Sports Hall of Fame two years later.

Bush

Bush was a Cardiff RFC stalwart and eventually racked up more than 170 appearances for the club, as well as being appointed captain. He only won eight caps for his country but he will be forever remembered as being in the side that beat the 1905 All Blacks in the epic match in Cardiff that was won by a solitary Teddy Morgan try.

The previous year, Bush had been selected to tour Australia and New Zealand with the British Isles and he played in all four Tests. He was so skilful and elusive that the Australian media christened him Will o' the Wisp, and the tourists dispatched the hosts comfortably in every game. On this leg of the tour he scored 12 tries, kicked the same number of conversions and also chipped in with four penalties and eight drop goals.

The second phase of the tour was more difficult and, despite winning their opening two games in New

LEFT Percy Bush

BUSH

Name: Percy Frank Bush
Born: 23rd June 1879, Cardiff, Wales
Died: 19th May 1955, Cardiff
Position: Fly-half
International Career: 1904 - 1910
International Caps: 12
International Points: 40
Honours: Home Nations Championship (1905, 1906, 1908, 1909), Grand Slam (1908, 1909)

BELOW The Wales team including Percy Bush (bottom row, far right)

Zealand, they then lost the all-important Test match. Overall, however, the tour was well received by the hosts and the matches were covered extensively in the media. Despite being a relatively new institution, the Lions were off to a good start.

When New Zealand arrived in Wales for their 1905 tour, Bush and the home side were a different proposition. He ran beautiful lines of attack and created the space for Morgan's crucial try in front of 47,000 in Cardiff. Kiwi Bobby Deans crossed for what he thought was a try that would have levelled the game at the death but the score was disallowed and Wales held on for the famous win.

Cardiff rocked South Africa 17-0 in appalling conditions in 1907 but Bush was no longer guaranteed a place in the national side following an 11-0 defeat to the Springboks at St Helen's in Swansea. He returned to form the following year, however, and was a valuable cog in the Triple Crown-winning team in 1908.

One of the most talented Welshmen of the pre-war era, Bush was also an accomplished cricketer.

Davies, Jonathan

Jonathan Davies was a gifted youngster but he left school at 17 to become a decorator. He first played for Trimsaran RFC but was then rejected by Llanelli. Neath gave him another chance and he signed as a fly-half in 1982. He played only 35 matches over the following two seasons but was then selected to play for Wales against England at the Arms Park. He scored a try and a drop goal on debut and was named man of the match. This was a lean period in Welsh rugby, however, and the side was expected to perform poorly at the inaugural World Cup in New Zealand in 1987.

ABOVE Jonathan Davies was a dual-code international

Wales shunned the formbook and won their three pool matches against Ireland, Canada and Tonga. They then beat England comfortably in Brisbane to set up a semi-final against New Zealand. It was a one-sided match that highlighted the inadequacies of the northern hemisphere game and Davies was critical of the Welsh attitude and preparation.

Despite the growing rift between him

and the WRFU, Davies guided Wales to a Triple Crown the following year, scoring a brilliant solo try against Scotland and wreaking havoc with the English defence. He took over the captaincy during the subsequent tour of New Zealand in the summer of 1988 and he was one of the few players to come home with their reputation intact after the Welsh were systematically dismantled by a fearsome All Black XV. Davies aired his views on what went wrong and made a number of recommendations to the management but they denied him a request to address the annual general meeting and the final straw was a 15-9 home defeat to Romania. With his relationship with the management soured, he eventually chose to join rugby league outfit Widnes for a record £230,000.

After a cautious start to his new career, Davies excelled in the alternate format and scored a wonderful solo try for Great Britain against Australia at Wembley in 1994. After 19 internationals for Wales and team GB he controversially returned to rugby union, although he struggled to readjust to a game that was in the throes of turning professional. He wasn't selected for the World Cup in South Africa in 1995 but did win five more caps before retiring after scoring eight points in Wales's 34-13 loss to England in the last Test match to be played at Cardiff Arms Park in 1997. England legends Will Carling and Rob Andrew hung up their boots the same day, but Davies was arguably the most skilful and electric of the three.

He may have been slight of build but Davies had an electrifying burst of pace, one of the game's great sidesteps and the vision to pick out the killer pass. He was awarded an MBE in 1996 and continues to commentate on both codes in English and Welsh.

Name: Jonathan Davies, MBE
Born: 24th October 1962, Carmarthenshire, Wales
Position: Fly-half
Height: 5'9" (1.75m)
Weight: 172lbs (78kg)
International Career: 1985 - 1997
International Caps: 32
International Points: 81
Honours: World Cup Third Place (1987), Five Nations Championship and Triple Crown (1988)

Davies, Mervyn

Davies attended Penlan School and was immediately earmarked as a future star. He played for London Welsh before moving home to join Swansea. He won his first cap for Wales against Scotland at the age of 23 and he soon developed a 'Merv the Swerve' nickname on account of his mazy runs.

He became a permanent fixture at number eight in the Welsh side and racked up 38 consecutive matches, during which he scored two tries. His mastery of the forward game saw him selected for the Lions tours to New Zealand in 1971, where he played all four Tests, and South Africa three years later, where he again played in every Test. Davies was a great reader of the game and he was often the target at the tail of the lineout. He was also quick and elusive at the rear of the scrum, and he was blessed with the superb handling skills of a basketball player.

The tours were a great success and this was mirrored in his performances for Wales. In 1975, Merv was given the national captaincy and a Grand Slam followed in only his second campaign at the helm. Although Davies injured his left calf during the early stages of the match at the Arms Park, he refused to go off as the French mounted a comeback and Wales clinched the championship with a 19-13 victory. Three weeks later, the Swansea star's career was ended after he suffered a

In 2001 he was inducted into the International Hall of Fame and the following year he was voted the best Welsh captain and number eight in the country's history.

DAVIES, MERVYN

BELOW Mervyn Davies of the British Lions in action during the 1974 tour of South Africa

brain haemorrhage in the Welsh Cup semi-final against Pontypool. The 29-year-old had surgery to save his life and made a miraculous recovery. By the time he retired, the national team had won two Grand Slams and three Triple Crowns with Davies at the back of the scrum, and in his 46 internationals he only lost nine times.

In 2001 he was inducted into the International Hall of Fame and the following year he was voted the best Welsh captain and number eight in the country's history, high praise indeed. A heavy smoker, Davies was diagnosed with lung cancer in 2011. The following year, the rugby world mourned the loss of one of its greatest exponents.

Name: Thomas Mervyn Davies, OBE
Born: 9th December 1946, Swansea, Wales
Died: 15th March 2012
Position: Number 8
Height: 6'5" (1.95m)
Weight: 238lbs (108kg)
International Career: 1969 - 1976
International Caps: 46
International Points: 7
Honours: Five Nations Championship (1969, 1970, 1971, 1973, 1975, 1976), Five Nations Grand Slam (1971, 1976), Lions Series Winner (1971, 1974)

Davies, Gerald

Davies was a promising schoolboy and was soon plying his trade at Loughborough and Cambridge University. He initially played with Cardiff and London Welsh, and he made his international debut in a rare defeat by Australia at the Arms Park in 1966. He moved from centre to wing for the Welsh tour of New Zealand in 1969, but this was only because he'd played in the position for the 1968 Lions on their tour of South Africa.

Davies was a brilliant running wing who could step off either foot and deliver killer passes from both hands. He cemented his reputation on the 1971 tour to New Zealand and will be forever linked with the all-conquering Welsh sides of the 1970s. His record is virtually unsurpassed: in only 46 internationals for his country he touched down 20 times, and he scored another three tries

ABOVE Gerald Davies of Wales runs with the ball during the Welsh tour to Australia

in five matches for the Lions, all of them on the 1971 tour. He was ranked alongside Gareth Edwards, Barry John, JPR and JJ Williams, Phil Bennett, Mervyn Davies, Graham Price and Bobby Windsor as one of the legendary Welsh players in the 1970s and he skippered the Barbarians against the Lions in the queen's jubilee match. He was the scorer of some of the most audacious and outrageous tries in rugby history and was the lynchpin in three Five Nations Grand Slams and five Triple Crowns during the most successful period in Welsh rugby history. He has since become a household name.

He retired in 1978 after a glittering career and turned his considerable talents to writing for the *Times*, sitting on the committee to reform Welsh rugby which had entered the doldrums in the 1980s and early 1990s, and devoting time to promoting youth rugby. In 2007 he was appointed as one of the managers for the 2009 Lions tour to South Africa.

Having been soundly beaten in 2005, the Lions needed to roar in 2009 and they didn't disappoint. Although they narrowly lost the first two Test matches, these titanic encounters paved the way for a heroic 28-9 win in the third Test in Johannesburg. Had a number of key players not been injured they could well have taken the series – indeed they led deep into injury time in the second Test.

Davies was a brilliant running wing who could step off either foot and deliver killer passes from both hands.

Name: Thomas Gerald Reames Davies, CBE
Born: 7th February 1945, Llansaint, Wales
Position: Wing
Height: 5'9" (1.74m)
Weight: 163 (74kg)
International Career: 1966 - 1978
International Caps: 51
International Points: 81
Honours: Five Nations Championship (1966, 1969, 1970, 1971, 1973, 1975, 1976, 1978), Five Nations Grand Slam (1971, 1976, 1978), Lions Series Winner (1971, 1974)

Dawes

Dawes was educated at Lewis School, the University of Wales and Loughborough. He gained a degree in chemistry and a PGCE, and also played rugby for Newbridge before joining London Welsh.

He won his first international cap against Ireland in 1964 and his performances in the Five Nations saw him called up to the touring party of East Africa later that year. He went on to captain Wales and led them to a Grand Slam in 1971. This pushed him up the pecking order for those being considered for the Lions captaincy, and he was duly appointed before the New Zealand tour. Under the tutelage of Carwyn James, the side became the first – and so far only – Lions team to win a Test series against the All Blacks.

The first match in Dunedin was a tight affair but an Ian McLauchlan try and two penalties saw them scrape home 9-3. Some of the players became overconfident but they were brought down to earth after being on the end of a Kiwi backlash in the second Test. The All Blacks scored five tries to the Lions' two and stormed to a 22-12 victory in Christchurch. The third match in Wellington saw the tourists back to their best and they ran out easy winners, 13-3. If they drew or won the last Test in Auckland, the Lions would seal a historic series win.

It was 8-8 at halftime, with both sides scoring a try, conversion and penalty. And it was 11-11 going into the last 20 minutes when JPR Williams kicked a magnificent 45-metre drop goal, the only one of his career. The All Blacks rallied with a late penalty but could only draw the match.

Dawes followed on from this success by captaining the Barbarians at Cardiff Arms Park when they famously beat New Zealand 23-11 in 1973. He retired

the following year and coached the national side until 1979, a period during which Wales won the Five Nations Championship four times. He also coached the Lions on their tour back to New Zealand in 1977, although this trip wasn't as successful as the three-quarters lacked the pace and power to trouble the All Black backline.

He is now President of London Welsh and holds the distinction of never having lost to England, either as a player or coach, in his entire career.

Name: Sydney John Dawes, OBE
Born: 29th June 1940, Newbridge, Wales
Position: Centre
Height: 5'10" (1.78m)
Weight: 180lbs (82kg)
International Career: 1964 - 1971
International Caps: 26
International Points: 12
Honours: Five Nations Championship (1964, 1965, 1966, 1969, 1970, 1971), Five Nations Grand Slam (1971), Lions Series Winner (1971)

LEFT John Dawes before a Lions tour

Edwards

The son of a miner, Edwards was educated at Pontardawe Technical School. His sublime skills were spotted by sports teacher Bill Samuels who suggested he try for a sports scholarship to Millfield School in Somerset. He was an accomplished gymnast, athlete and footballer, and he signed for Swansea as a 16-year-old.

The lure of playing rugby for Wales at the beginning of their golden era in the late 1960s proved too much, however, and Edwards was handed his first cap in 1967 at the age of 20 against France in Paris. He was given the captaincy in 1968 and then played in a record 58 consecutive matches for his country, never suffering an injury or loss of form.

Edwards turned 21 on his first Lions tour to South Africa in 1968. His half-back partnership with Barry John was still in its infancy and the team were not good enough to trouble their hosts. However, in New Zealand three years later, the pairing were at their devastating best. As long as rugby is played, the argument will rage over which of the 1971 and 1974 sides was better but Edwards undoubtedly played the key role in both successes. He was the best scrum-half of the era – perhaps of any era – and his devastating breaks, elusive running and fine distribution edged the series for the Lions. Although he was forced off the field with a leg injury during the first Test, he returned for the remainder of the series and produced his finest performance in the third match when his break opened the All Black defence down the blindside and he created a try for Gerald Davies.

ABOVE Gareth Edwards (left) and Phil Bennett

He was the best scrum-half of the era – perhaps of any era.

In 1973, Edwards scored the greatest try in the history of the game when he finished off a move started by Phil Bennett in his own 25. It was a score of breathtaking beauty and it ensured the Barbarians beat the mighty All Blacks in Cardiff, 23-11. "The game against the All Blacks is one I will never forget, and those of us who played in it will never be allowed to forget," Edwards said later.

The match was just a few minutes old when Edwards rounded off the move after the ball passed through eight pairs of hands. Cliff Morgan's commentary is as unforgettable as the try itself: "This is great stuff. Phil Bennett covering. Chased by Alasdair Scown. Brilliant! Oh, that's brilliant! John Williams. Brian Williams. Pullin. John Dawes, great dummy. David, Tom David. The halfway line. Brilliant by Quinnell! This is Gareth Edwards! A dramatic start! What a score! Oh, that fellow Edwards."

In South Africa a year later, Edwards was at his peak. His forwards destroyed the Springbok pack and allowed him so much time and space that he could control the pace of the game single-handedly. He slotted the decisive drop goal in the first Test and delivered a pinpoint reverse pass for Phil Bennett to seal the series win with another drop. Willie John McBride promptly described him as the best scrum-half he had ever seen or was ever likely to see, high praise indeed from the legendary Lion. His outstanding contribution to the tour led to him being awarded the 1974 BBC Sports Personality of the Year.

Name: Gareth Owen Edwards, CBE
Born: 12th July 1947, Pontardawe, Wales
Position: Scrum-half
Height: 5'8" (1.73m)
Weight: 165lbs (75kg)
International Career: 1967 - 1978
International Caps: 63
International Points: 91
Honours: Five Nations Championship (1969, 1970, 1971, 1973, 1975, 1976, 1978), Five Nations Grand Slam (1971, 1976, 1978), Lions Series Winner (1971, 1974)

He was equally impressive in the Five Nations, winning the championship seven times and recording three Grand Slams. He retired in 1978 and was immediately back in the spotlight when he became captain on A Question of Sport. In 1997 he was one of the first inductees into the Hall of Fame, and in 2001 he was voted the greatest Welsh player of all time.

Edwards showcased new skills to the world when he retired from rugby and represented Wales at angling. He promptly set a British record when he landed a 45lb pike at Llandegfedd Reservoir near Pontypool. He has contributed to a number of books on rugby and fishing, plays golf, shoots and commentates on the game for Welsh language channel S4C.

It's unusual to finish a piece on Edwards with a contribution from an Englishman but former England captain Will Carling summed up his impact on the game thus: "Edwards was a supreme athlete with supreme skills. His running, passing, kicking and reading of the game were outstanding and he sits astride the whole of planet rugby."

In 2003 Rugby World magazine voted Edwards the greatest player of all time.

BELOW Gareth Edwards celebrates a Lions try

Evans

Evans's rugby career began at the Queen Elizabeth Grammar School and then Carmarthen Quins. He joined Llanelli at the age of 19 and eventually played in seven cup finals for the team, of which they won five, this despite almost having his career ended by a serious ankle injury. He then joined Bath and helped the side to the 1998 European Cup.

His international career was equally glittering. He made his debut for Wales in Paris in 1987 and proved himself a winger with great speed and skill later that year in the inaugural World Cup, at which Wales finished third after late wins over England and Australia. He scored a brilliant solo try against Scotland during the Triple Crown-winning season of 1988 and often stood in as captain thereafter.

He was selected for the Lions tour to Australia in 1989 and scored the decisive try in the third Test after a mistake by David Campese. He also scored a magnificent try against England at the Arms Park in 1993 and captained Wales to the Five Nations Championship the following year.

The 1991 World Cup defeat to Western Samoa may have been the lowest point in his international career but his second Lions tour showed he was still at the peak of his powers and he was the tourists' top scorer with four tries. He couldn't help them to a series win, however, but he was back with the team in South Africa four years later. Although more of a fringe player towards the end of his career, he still helped the Lions to victory over the world champions. (The 1995 World Cup had been another disappointment as Wales had failed to qualify from their group after a narrow loss to Ireland in their final match.)

Evans retired at the end of the fol-

RIGHT Ieuan Evans of the Lions rounds Eroni Clarke of Auckland to score

lowing season but his record stands up against the best in the game: 72 caps for his country – of which 28 were as captain – and 33 tries puts him third on the Welsh all-time list behind only Shane Williams and Gareth Thomas.

He was awarded the MBE for services to the sport in 1996, and in 2007 he was inducted into the International Rugby Hall of Fame. He now works as a pundit for Sky TV's *The Rugby Club* and runs his own PR company.

Name: Ieuan Cennydd Evans, MBE
Born: 21st March 1964, Pontardulais, Wales
Position: Wing
Height: 5'10" (1.78m)
Weight: 187lbs (85kg)
International Career: 1987 - 1998
International Caps: 79
International Points: 162
Honours: World Cup Third Place (1987), Five Nations Triple Crown (1988), Lions Series Winner (1989), Five Nations Championship (1994)

Gibbs

Scott Gibbs will perhaps unfairly be remembered for two magic moments, the first a crunching hit on South African prop Os du Randt in the second Test of the 1997 Lions tour in Durban, and the second a jinking run to silence England in the last Five Nations match at Wembley in 1999. But Gibbs was much more than a two-hit wonder.

The slight centre started his career at Pencoed RFC and he soon graduated to senior rugby with Bridgend. He was capped by his country in 1991 but he needed a higher class of club rugby if his career was going to progress. He joined Swansea and had an immediate impact, helping himself to a hatful of tries and the club to the 1992 cup final at the Arms Park (they eventually lost to Llanelli).

Despite being only 22 he was selected for the 1993 Lions tour to New Zealand and he raised a few eyebrows by being picked for the team in the second and third Tests ahead of England captain Will Carling. He justified his place in the side, however, and was one of the stars of the tour.

There was criticism over his size though, so he spent several years bulking up with rugby league outfit St Helens. As the union code went professional, Gibbs flitted between the two, playing for Wales at the 1995 World Cup and then helping St Helens to the Challenge Cup and Super League titles the following year.

The 1997 Lions tour to South Africa was a success on every level and Gibbs's bullocking run and huge hit on du Randt lifted the entire squad. He was later voted player of the series. His Wembley try two years later sank England by a point, denying them the championship and handing the title to Scotland. Wales were trailing against

LEFT Scott Gibbs in action

Name: Ian Scott Gibbs
Born: 23rd January 1971, Bridgend, Wales
Position: Centre
Height: 5'9" (1.75m)
Weight: 217lbs (98kg)
International Career: 1991 - 2001
International Caps: 58
International Points: 55
Honours: Lions Series Winner (1997)

the Grand Slam-chasing favourites but time was running out for the visitors in the last ever Five Nations match. Chris Wyatt won a lineout just inside the English half and the Welsh half-backs slipped the ball to Gibbs. The big centre left a sea of English defenders in his wake as he jinked his way to the try-line to provide the perfect finish. Neil Jenkins still needed to convert the score to give Wales victory but 'The Boot' casually knocked over the pressure kick and dashed England's hopes.

Gibbs was again selected for Lions duty on the 2001 tour to Australia but by then he was past his best and he didn't play in the Test team. He was appointed captain of Neath-Swansea Ospreys when Welsh professional rugby went regional in the summer of 2003, but he quit the sport five months later to concentrate on his role as development manager with Liberty Properties Plc.

This exceptional centre with a great turn of speed, huge presence and mischievous personality retired from international duty with 53 Welsh caps, although he occasionally returns to our screens with the BBC. He now lives in South Africa.

Gould

Arthur Gould was born into a family of athletes and his male siblings were all accomplished rugby players (Bob captained the national side in 1887, Bert won the Triple Crown in 1893 and Harry, Gus and Wyatt all played for Newport). Arthur was also a fine sprinter who finished third in the national championship hurdles in 1887 and 1893.

He made his first appearance for Newport when the regular fullback went to a funeral. Despite his lack of experience, Gould scored two of his side's three tries and thereafter he was never dropped by the captain until he retired 16 years later in 1898. The game was strictly amateur so he travelled the country as a public contractor and often turned out for provincial sides. He returned to Newport for their unbeaten 1891-92 season and ran in 37 tries in 24 matches, a record that still stands. Over the next eight years and 231 appearances, he scored 159 tries.

He first represented Wales for their Home Nations Championship encounter with England in 1885. Playing alongside brother Bob, the side narrowly lost and could

He was the game's first superstar, one who bridged the gap between sport and celebrity.... the most gifted and accomplished player of his generation.

then only draw with Scotland. The national team experimented with playing four three-quarters but the tactic didn't work and Wales underperformed for the next two years.

Gould was given the captaincy in 1889 and he scored his first international try the following season. The side still struggled for consistency and it wasn't until 1893 that a settled Wales finally delivered, winning the Triple Crown and the championship. Gould scored a memorable try from the halfway line against England and then ran in another late on to seal the victory.

Name: Arthur Joseph Gould
Born: 10th October 1864, Newport, Wales
Died: 2nd January 1919, Newport
Position: Fullback / Centre
Height: 5'10" (1.79m)
Weight: 154lbs (70kg)
International Career: 1885 - 1897
International Caps: 27
International Points: 13
Honours: Home Unions Championship (1888, 1893)

The home nations quickly adopted the Welsh running style and their greater resources saw them overhaul Gould's side. He retired in 1896 but was lured back for the 1897 championship. Wales then left the IRB after trying to organise his testimonial. As this meant paying the player for his contribution to the game, that would constitute professionalism, which was illegal.

The affair rumbled on and soured the end of a brilliant career. Indeed Gould was a national hero who was as well known and revered as WG Grace. Wales were eventually readmitted into the IRB the following year, by which time Gould had become a respected referee.

When he died in 1919, his funeral was the largest ever held in Wales. He was the game's first superstar, one who bridged the gap between sport and celebrity, and he was doubtless the most gifted and accomplished player of his generation.

LEFT Arthur Gould wearing his Welsh jersey and international cap in 1897

Halfpenny

Leigh Halfpenny was spotted as a potential international while still at school. He was signed as a youth by Neath Swansea Ospreys as a wing or fullback and enjoyed one season with the side before signing for the Cardiff Blues. He was such a talent that he was drafted into the national squad for their match against South Africa in the 2008 autumn series.

He scored a penalty on debut but couldn't prevent the Welsh losing 15-20 to the world champions. He scored his first two tries in the next match of the series against Canada and backed this up with more solid performances in the 2009 Six Nations, although he was then dropped by Warren Gatland in favour of Mark Jones. He scored two tries for Cardiff in the final of the EDF Cup and was selected to tour with the Lions to South Africa that summer.

He missed the start of the tour with a thigh injury and only returned for the match against the Free State Cheetahs, but the injury recurred and Halfpenny had to withdraw from the squad. He suffered more injury problems in the build-up to the 2011 World Cup in New Zealand but was on superb form during the tournament itself and would have taken Wales to the final had his last-minute penalty from 45 metres not fallen inches short.

He was the standout player during the 2012 Six Nations and finished the tournament as the top scorer. His late penalty secured a two-point win over Ireland and he scored another 14 points to see off England and claim the Grand Slam. After superb performances against France and Italy in the 2013 Six Nations campaign – both of which earned him the man-of-the-match nomination – he was voted the best player in the tournament and was selected for the Lions tour to Australia.

LEFT Leigh Halfpenny at the post-match celebration following Wales's 2012 Grand Slam

Halfpenny was the catalyst for all the Lions' best moves, and he was instrumental in the tourists' wins in the first and last Tests that secured the series. He only missed four kicks during the entire tour and broke Neil Jenkins's scoring record with 49 points from the three games. He was voted man of the series and was shortlisted for the World Player of the Year honours. He also finished runner-up to Andy Murray at the prestigious BBC Sports Personality of the Year awards.

He kicked two conversions and three penalties as Wales beat Italy in their opening match of the 2014 Six Nations but they were soundly beaten by Ireland in their second game. Halfpenny was inspired in the 27-6 win over France, however, converting Sam Warburton's try and adding another five penalties to give them a comfortable win. He kicked six penalties against England but dislocated his shoulder towards the end of the match.

Halfpenny returned for the autumn internationals but Wales lost to Australia and New Zealand before finishing the series with a flourish with a rare win over South Africa. He was outstanding in the 2015 Six Nations but the Welsh loss to England denied them a Grand Slam and they eventually finished third in the championship.

Name: Stephen Leigh Halfpenny
Born: 22nd December 1988, Gorseinon, Wales
Position: Fullback / Wing
Height: 5'10" (1.78m)
Weight: 187lbs (85kg)
International Career: 2008 - present
International Caps: 63
International Points: 531
Honours: Six Nations Championship and Grand Slam (2008, 2012), Lions Series Winner (2013)

Howley

Howley played for local side Bridgend before joining Cardiff. He was handed his national debut in 1996 against England and scored a brilliant try. He backed this up with another solo effort after an arcing run around the entire French defence in Cardiff. Such was his impact at international level that he was selected for the 1997 Lions tour to South Africa. His personal duel with Springbok legend Joost van der Westhuizen was one of the most eagerly anticipated match-ups of the series but Howley picked up a shoulder injury and was ruled out of the Tests. It was a bitter blow for a player who was fast-becoming the standout scrum-half in world rugby.

Howley helped Wales defeat England at Wembley in the last Five Nations encounter in 1999 but this was largely a barren period in Welsh rugby and they made little impact in the final standings. Despite a surprising loss to Samoa, Wales topped their group at that year's World Cup and Howley scored a try in the 64-15 demolition of Japan. Australia were too strong in the quarter-final, however, and Wales were eliminated.

On a personal level, Howley was on such good form for the next two seasons that he was picked for the Lions on their 2001 tour to Australia. He played in the first two Tests but picked up another injury and missed the decisive third Test, which the tourists lost.

He moved from Cardiff to London Wasps but a wrist injury curtailed his career and he announced his retirement after winning the Heineken Cup in 2004. Had it not been for bad luck and this spate of injuries, Howley would now be remembered as one of the game's great number nines. As it is, two Lions tours, 59 caps for his country, of which 22 were as captain, and 10 Test tries still see him ranked by his peers as

RIGHT Rob Howley is now head coach of Wales

...Howley would now be remembered as one of the game's great number nines.

a scrum-half of real talent.

He worked with the Wales squad as an assistant coach in the build-up to the 2013 Six Nations Championship but took over the head coach's role before their opening fixture against Ireland. He then travelled to Australia with the Lions in a coaching capacity. Having been so unlucky with injuries as a player, Howley was finally rewarded with a 2-1 series victory.

Name: Robert Howley
Born: 13th October 1970, Bridgend, Wales
Position: Scrum-half
Height: 5'9" (1.75m)
Weight: 187lbs (85kg)
International Career: 1996 - 2002
International Caps: 61
International Points: 50
Honours: Two Lions Tours (1997, 2001), World Cup Quarter-final (1999), Lions Tour Winner as Coach (2013)

Jenkins, Gethin

Gethin Jenkins didn't play rugby until he was 13 but he soon joined youth side Treorchy. Having had a brief spell with rugby league outfit Cardiff Demons, Jenkins signed for Pontypridd in 2001 and was called up to the national squad for their match against Romania the following year. This was a time when Welsh rugby was still adapting to professionalism, however, and, with two minor exceptions, the side had been in the international wilderness since finishing third at the 1987 World Cup.

Steve Hansen took over as coach in 2002 and Wales reinvented their fluid attacking style for the 2003 World Cup. They may have lost to New Zealand and England but their entertaining brand of running rugby won them many admirers and they soon converted this promise into silverware.

They edged past England in the opening match of the 2005 Six Nations and then thumped Italy 38-8. Beating France in Paris proved to be the acid test as Wales easily brushed past Scotland before beating Ireland in the championship decider to claim the long-awaited Grand Slam (Jenkins scored the opening try in the last match).

The next two campaigns were disappointing and Wales could only manage one win in each tournament. They also failed to qualify from their group at the 2007 World Cup and suddenly the Grand Slam triumph of 2005 seemed a distant memory. Jenkins captained the side for a game against South Africa in the autumn series and remained the first name on the team sheet for the glorious return to form in the 2008 Six Nations. Wales won away at Twickenham and Croke Park to secure Jenkins his second Grand Slam.

Wales finished mid-table in 2009 but Jenkins was still the standout forward and he toured South Africa with the

Lions later in the year. It was an epic series that the hosts edged 2-1. Wales were uncharacteristically poor in the subsequent Six Nations and only managed five wins in their next two campaigns, but Jenkins then became one of only six players to win three Grand Slams in 2012, and he also captained the side again in the last match of the 2013 Six Nations. Wales's 30-3 demolition of England secured him his fourth title. In November, he became his country's most-capped forward when he made his 101st appearance.

In the 2014 Six Nations, Wales could only finish in third place behind Ireland and England, but Jenkins once again took the captain's armband for the autumn international series that saw Wales beat South Africa and Fiji. He was also the cornerstone of a pack that won four of their five matches in the 2015 Six Nations.

ABOVE Gethin Jenkins

Name: Gethin Jenkins
Born: 17th November 1980, Llantwit Fardre, Wales
Position: Prop
Height: 6'2" (1.88m)
Weight: 265lbs (120kg)
International Career: 2002 - present
International Caps: 119
International Points: 20
Honours: Six Nations Championship (2005, 2008, 2012, 2013), Six Nations Grand Slam (2005, 2008, 2012)

Jenkins, Neil

Jenkins was a schoolboy player of some talent but it wasn't until a move to Ponypridd in 1990 that he became known to a wider audience. Good performances at fly-half and fullback saw him selected for Wales the following season, although the side was comprehensively outplayed by England in Cardiff and Jenkins missed out on selection for the World Cup squad.

Despite coming in for criticism over his perceived lack of pace and his preference for kicking, Jenkins worked on his all-round game and was soon the best distributor of flat passes to the backline and he repeatedly opened up defences. His goal-kicking was second to none and he was his country's record points scorer before making his 30th start.

He was selected as a utility player for the 1997 Lions in South Africa but proved his worth by keeping the scoreboard ticking over and pegging the Springboks back with his precise kicking. The tourists secured the series win, and Jenkins was on hand again for his country when he notched the crucial conversion to beat England at Wembley. This was a period of transition for Welsh rugby, however, and it wasn't until Steve Hansen took over from Graham Henry in 2002 that their fortunes improved.

In 2001 Jenkins became the first man to score 1,000 international points, and later that year he was selected for the Lions tour to Australia. He played

In 2001 Jenkins became the first man to score 1,000 international points

second fiddle to Jonny Wilkinson but did come on late in the second Test. He was omitted from Wales's 2003 World Cup squad and retired from the game. His 44 consecutive goal-kicks remains a world record, and his 1,090 international points sees him third on the all-time list behind Dan Carter and Wilkinson.

In 2004, Jenkins became the kicking coach for the national team, and he was also the skills coach during the 2008 Grand Slam. He toured South Africa with the 2009 Lions in the same capacity but the visitors narrowly lost an enthralling series.

Name: Neil Roger Jenkins, MBE
Born: 8th July 1971, Church Village, Wales
Position: Fullback
Height: 5'10" (1.78m)
Weight: 190lbs (86kg)
International Career: 1991 - 2002
International Caps: 91
International Points: 1,090
Honours: Five Nations Champions (1994), Lions Series Winner (1997)

Neil Jenkins kicks a penalty

John, Barry

The supremely talented but diminutive Welshman was rugby's George Best, the game's first global superstar. He didn't have the size to intimidate opponents but he made up for his physical shortcomings with a sensational sidestep off both feet, precise kicking and crisp passing. With Gareth Edwards inside him, this was perhaps the finest midfield pairing in the game's history.

John was lucky to be schooled in the sport's finer points by William Jones and Ray Williams, and it was while at grammar school that he made his first appearance for Llanelli in a match against Moseley. He was first capped by Wales in 1966 but his international career started slowly and he had to wait until the 1968 Lions tour before he emerged on the world stage.

The eagerly awaited battle with the Springboks' back row on John's first Lions tour ended 15 minutes into the first Test, however. John made a darting break for the line but was hauled down by Ellis and broke his collarbone on the hard ground.

This was a golden age for Welsh rugby and they won the Triple Crown in 1969 before sharing the championship with France the following year. The 1971 Five Nations campaign was one of the most emphatic in history: John scored two drop-goals as Wales demolished England 22-6 in Cardiff in their opening game; he then scored a try and conversion against Scotland in a narrow win; he added a conversion, two penalties and another drop in a 23-9 victory over Ireland; and he then scored a try and a penalty to beat France in the last match to secure the historic Grand Slam.

Later in the year, the rugby world was treated to breathtaking performances as Edwards and John were again pitted against the best from the southern

RIGHT Barry John kicks the 1971 Lions to victory in New Zealand

hemisphere. In what was their annus mirabilis, the pair guided the Lions to their only series win to date over the All Blacks. Their self-confidence bordered on arrogance but this infectious enthusiasm permeated the entire squad and they ripped the provincial sides to shreds. John masterminded the 47-9 annihilation of champions Wellington and scored a try of such beauty against a collective university side that the crowd was completely silenced. He finished the tour with 30 of the Lions' 48 Test points.

Scotland and Wales refused to travel to Ireland after the events of Bloody Sunday so the 1972 Five Nations Championship remained unresolved. Wales won their three games with John contributing two penalties and conversion against England, three more penalties and another three conversions against Scotland, and four penalties against France. In so doing, John became his country's leading international scorer.

Then, while at the peak of his powers, he decided to retire at the age of just 27. The weight of expectation for club and country was proving too much and he felt like he was living in a goldfish bowl. The rugby world was denied this mercurial talent, although his magical individual performances, goal-kicking records and peerless displays with both Wales and the Lions have cemented his god-like status to everyone who saw him play.

Not for nothing was Barry John known as 'The King'.

Name: Barry John
Born: 6th January 1945, Cefneithin, Wales
Position: Fly-half
Height: 5'10" (1.78m)
Weight: 165lbs (75kg)
International Career: 1966 - 1972
International Caps: 30
International Points: 120
Honours: Five Nations Championship (1966, 1969, 1970, 1971), Five Nations Grand Slam (1971), Lions Series Winner (1971)

John, Roy

John represented his local grammar school and showed such agility, pace and a deft sidestep for a big man that he joined Neath in his late teens. He made his international debut against England in the 1950 Five Nations but the team was expected to perform poorly as a number of new caps had been added to bolster a weak squad.

They beat England and then swept the other nations aside to complete a historic Grand Slam (they only conceded eight points in their four games). John had scored in the final match against France and he was selected for the 1950 Lions tour on the back of these solid performances. Together with club-mate Rees Stephens, they toiled away in the engine room for 22 tour matches, including all six Tests. They won two against Australia but only one of the four against New Zealand.

He was a regular in the Welsh squad for the next three Five Nations campaigns and helped the side to a second Grand Slam in 1952. England led by six points during the crucial first match in London but John began to dominate the lineout and Wales fought back to win by two. They shut Scotland out the following week and then beat Ireland by

Name: Ernest Raymond 'Roy' John
Born: 3rd December 1925, Crynant, Wales
Died: 30th September 1981, Neath
Position: Lock / Number 8
Height: 6'2" (1.88m)
Weight: 191lbs (87kg)
International Career: 1950 - 1954
International Caps: 25
International Points: 6
Honours: Five Nations Championship (1950, 1952, 1954), Five Nations Grand Slam (1950, 1952)

RIGHT Roy John

Such agility, pace and a deft sidestep for a big man...

11 points. A tight win over France in Swansea made John a household name and he would have joined the other immortals with three Grand Slams had England not won in Cardiff in 1953.

He played his final international against the old enemy in 1954 and retired after 19 consecutive appearances. His finest moment came in his penultimate game, however, when Wales scored a rare victory over the touring All Blacks.

Jones, Adam

Jones joined the Ospreys from Neath in 2003 and made his international debut as a substitute against England during that season's Six Nations. Steve Hansen had only just taken the reins as national coach and the side forged a reputation for brilliant counterattacking rugby at the 2003 World Cup. Wales returned from the international wilderness with outstanding displays against New Zealand and eventual champions England, albeit in losing causes.

Jones was initially criticised for a lack of fitness and poor mobility but he silenced the doubters with a solid 2004 Six Nations and then a long-awaited Grand Slam the following season. Sir Clive Woodward inexplicably overlooked him for the disastrous Lions tour to New Zealand later that year and the fortunes of the national side also declined, culminating in an embarrassing exit at the 2007 World Cup. Jones was dropped for the vital game against Fiji and the islanders caused a huge upset in Nantes.

The Welsh rollercoaster took them from rock bottom to dizzying heights as the side regrouped and won an improbable Six Nations Grand Slam in 2008. He was the cornerstone of the pack under Warren Gatland and was selected by the Lions for the 2009 tour of South Africa. When Jones, Gethin Jenkins and Matthew Rees started the pivotal second Test against the Springboks it marked the first time an all-Welsh front row had started a Lions match since Billy Williams, Bryn Meredith and Courtney Meredith had fronted up against the same opposition in 1955. The Lions lost the match by three points and Jones was sent home after dislocating a shoulder.

He didn't return for Wales until the 2010 Six Nations but Wales only managed to beat Scotland and Italy. The

2011 campaign was equally disappointing and the side entered the World Cup in New Zealand with modest expectations. Wales then surprised themselves and everybody else by only losing one pool game (to South Africa by a point) and then seeing off a much-fancied Irish side 22-10 in the quarter-final. Had Jones not injured a calf, Sam Warburton not been harshly sent off and James Hook not missed two kickable penalties in the semi-final against France, Wales would have made the final against the hosts.

Jones was back to his best for the Six Nations Grand Slam in 2012 and the championship win the following season. He was also selected for the victorious 2013 Lions tour to Australia.

ABOVE Adam Rhys Jones

Name: Adam Rhys Jones
Born: 8th March 1981, Abercrave, Wales
Position: Prop
Height: 6' (1.83m)
Weight: 265lbs (120kg)
International Career: 2003 - 2015
International Caps: 100
International Points: 10
Honours: Five Nations Championship (2005, 2008, 2012, 2013), Five Nations Grand Slam (2005, 2008, 2012), Lions Series Winner (2013)

Jones, Lewis

Lewis Jones first played rugby at school and he then joined Neath. After serving in the navy he moved to Llanelli and was called up for Wales in their 1950 Five Nations match with England. Wales won by six points and went on to secure a historic Grand Slam after victories over Scotland and France in Cardiff, and Ireland in Dublin. He was then asked to join the Lions tour of Australia and New Zealand after injury had ruled out several players from the Test side.

He made an immediate impact, scoring 63 points in his seven matches in New Zealand and another 16 against Australia in Brisbane. He was instrumental in Wales's second Grand Slam in three years when they took the 1952 Five Nations Championship after a final victory over the French in Swansea. Realising he could cash in on his ability and fame, Jones signed for Leeds rugby league at the end of the year. He didn't take long to settle in and scored 302 points in only his second season (his record of more than 1,000 goals remained a Leeds record until Kevin Sinfield surpassed it in 2009).

He played for Great Britain 15 times and scored in every match, which included the 1957 World Cup in Australia where the side finished as runners up to the hosts. His performances in the tournament saw him hailed as one of the game's greats while still only in his early 20s. He equalled Jim Sullivan's Leeds club record of 496 points during the 1956-57 campaign but he spent another seven seasons with the club and eventually scored 3,372 career points. He then helped the Yorkshire side to their first championship in 1960-61.

Following six successful seasons as a player-coach with an Australian second-division side, Jones returned

RIGHT Lewis Jones

to Leeds in 1970 to teach. He was described by rugby historian Robert Gate as "Arguably the most devastating attacking back Wales has ever produced. His acceleration over the first few yards was stunning, allowing him to penetrate almost any defence and enabling him, in the mid 1950s, to become the greatest star in the game."

His book, *King of Rugger*, was published in 1958. He is one of the few players to be honoured by both codes and remains one of the finest exponents in the games' history. In 2013, this supremely gifted runner was inducted into the Rugby League Hall of Fame.

Name: Benjamin Lewis Jones
Born: 11th April 1931, Swansea, Wales
Position: Fullback / Centre / Wing
Height: 5'8" (1.73m)
Weight: 161lbs (73kg)
International Career: 1950 - 1952
International Caps: 13
International Points: 62
Honours: Five Nations Championship and Grand Slam (1950, 1952)

Jones, Ken

Jones was a student at West Monmouth Grammar School and he developed into a player of considerable skill and blistering pace. He concentrated on his sprinting while serving in the army during the war and he was selected for the sprint relay team at the 1948 Olympic Games in London. He collected a silver medal and then joined Newport RFC (he would later win bronze in the Commonwealth Games 220 yards in Vancouver and captain the British team at the European Championships in Berne).

By now he was a regular in the Welsh national side and he was soon running in tries from all parts of the field, but an uncharacteristic error in the last match of the 1949 championship allowed France to score a try and condemn Wales to the wooden spoon. He was back to his best in 1950 and his scores, which included tries against Scotland, Ireland and a brace against France, ensured that they won their first Grand Slam since 1911.

He didn't always get the service his class merited when playing for club or country but that changed on the 1950 Lions tour to Australia and New Zealand. He ran in 17 tries in 17 matches and played in three of the four Tests against the Kiwis. He scored a magnificent solo try in the fourth Test and was about to touchdown for the winner when the ball bounced awkwardly and eluded him.

If 1951 brought a downturn in the fortunes of the national team, 1952 saw the Welsh roar with pride and Jones scored tries against the three other home unions. His two tries against England secured their second Grand Slam in three seasons. The most famous try of a glittering career came in the dying minutes of Wales's epic 1953 encounter with the touring All Blacks who were thus far unbeaten. With the sides level, Clem Thomas delivered a perfect cross-

RIGHT Ken Jones touches down to score a try before England's William Hook can tackle him

field kick for Jones to gather. He then rounded Ron Jarden for the winning score, which remains the last time that Wales beat the mighty Kiwis.

He retired from international rugby in 1957 with 44 Welsh caps (then a world record) and 51 points under his belt. He was the inaugural winner of the Welsh Sports Personality of the Year and picked up an OBE in 1960. He was also the first rugby union inductee into the Welsh Sports Hall of Fame.

He died at the age of 84 in 2006.

Name: Kenneth Jeffrey 'Ken' Jones, OBE
Born: 30th December 1921, Blaenavon, Wales
Died: 18th April 2006, Newport
Position: Wing
Height: 5'11" (1.80m)
Weight: 172lbs (78kg)
International Career: 1947 - 1957
International Caps: 49
International Points: 65
Honours: Five Nations Championship (1947, 1950, 1952, 1954, 1955, 1956), Five Nations Grand Slam (1950, 1952)

Jones, Robert

Jones made his debut for Swansea as a teenager and he was soon being mentioned in the same breath as the Welsh greats of the past. He formed a formidable half-back partnership with Jonathan Davies before the stand-off switched codes and joined rugby league outfit Widnes, although they both played an important part in Wales's 1988 Triple Crown. In the match against Scotland, Jones flung an enormous reverse pass to Davies, with the latter then chipping through to score. He also supplied the key passes for Davies's two drop goals that sealed the match.

Jones was promptly chosen to tour Australia with the Lions, during which he arguably got the better of Wallaby legend Nick Farr-Jones. The Lions secured a 2-1 series win and Jones was ever-present for Wales in the next Five Nations on the back of his performances. He toured again with the Lions to New Zealand in 1993 – in what would be the last amateur series – but he didn't play a major role and couldn't help the team overcome the All Blacks in the Tests.

Jones retired from international rugby in 1995 having played 54 times for Wales and three times for the Lions. He was an accomplished and technical scrum-half with a killer pass, deft hands and a quick

Name: Robert Nicholas Jones
Born: 10th November 1965, Trebanos, Wales
Position: Scrum-half
Height: 5'8" (1.73m)
Weight: 162lbs (73kg)
International Career: 1986 - 1995
International Caps: 57
International Points: 19
Honours: Five Nations Triple Crown (1988), Lions Series Winner (1989), Five Nations Championship (1994)

RIGHT Robert Jones distributes the ball on the successful 1989 Lions tour of Australia

turn of pace around the ruck. He hung up his boots in 2001 but he can still be heard commentating on BBC radio and works as an assistant coach at Llanelli.

Jones, Ryan

Ryan Jones initially showed promise as a goalkeeper and played at junior level for Bristol City. Having discovered rugby at the age of 17, he soon became captain of Cardiff Metropolitan University and he then signed for Newport for a single appearance. He moved first to Bridgend and then to Celtic Warriors before signing with the Ospreys in 2004 (he was made club captain in 2007).

Having made his international debut against South Africa in 2004, which ended in an agonising 38-36 defeat, Jones was ever-present in the side that secured Wales their first Six Nations Grand Slam in 27 years the following season. He scored perhaps the try of the tournament against Scotland but was a surprise omission from Sir Clive Woodward's 2005 Lions tour of New Zealand. He was scheduled to travel with Wales to North America but received a late call-up to join the Lions after Simon Taylor picked up an injury. He was the standout player in the mid-week side's 30-19 victory over Otago and came on as a replacement in the first Test. Although the All Blacks won the series comfortably, Jones started the final two Tests and was one of the few players to return home with his reputation intact.

He was injured for much of 2006 and also missed the 2007 World cup. New coach Warren Gatland gave him the national captaincy in 2008 and Wales promptly delivered a second Grand Slam in four years. After a solid autumn series in which Wales only just lost to the world champion South Africans and New Zealand but then beat Canada and Australia, Jones was shortlisted for the World Player of the Year award.

He was again a late call-up for the 2009 Lions tour of South Africa but had to return home on medical advice after exacerbating a head injury. The follow-

RIGHT Ryan Jones after Wales's 2012 Grand Slam

In 2008 Jones was shortlisted for the World Player of the Year award.

ing seasons were littered with highs (a World Cup semi-final in 2011) and lows (a heavy defeat to France in the Six Nations) and it wasn't until 2012 that Wales delivered their third Grand Slam of the new millennium. Jones became his country's most-capped captain (33) later that year and the side defended its Six Nations title in 2013.

Name: Ryan Paul Jones
Born: 13th March 1981, Newport, Wales
Position: Number 8 / Flanker / Lock
Height: 6'5" (1.96m)
Weight: 251lbs (114kg)
International Career: 2004 - present
International Caps: 78
International Points: 10
Honours: Six Nations Championship (2005, 2008, 2012, 2013), Six Nations Grand Slam (2005, 2008, 2012)

Matthews

Matthews formed half of a legendary Welsh midfield with Bleddyn Williams. He was also a devastating tackler for such a small man. Born in Bridgend, South Wales, in 1920, Matthews attended the County School before heading for the University of Cardiff. He was short but powerfully built and quick, and he won the Welsh AAA 220 yards in 1937. A year later he was given a senior Welsh trial, and the year after that he came second in the Senior Men's 100 yards.

His career was interrupted by the war – which robbed him of his best years as an athlete – but he was commissioned into the medical corps and also learned to box. He famously held the future undefeated world champion Rocky Marciano to a three-round draw while the American was stationed in Wales with the 150th Combat Engineers, and he then resumed his rugby career with a win over France. The national side would go on to record a historic Grand Slam in 1950, with Matthews and Bleddyn Williams forming one of the game's greatest centre partnerships.

He played six Test matches for the Lions on the tour of Australia and New Zealand later that year, earning the nicknames 'Iron Man', 'Bulldozer' and 'Brick Wall' for his brutal tackling and confrontational demeanour. He finished his international career in 1951 having been capped 17 times by Wales and six times by the Lions. He also joined the

...Earning the nicknames 'Iron Man', 'Bulldozer' and 'Brick Wall' for his brutal tackling.

Name: Jack Matthews, OBE
Born: 21st June 1920, Bridgend, Wales
Died: 18th July 2012
Position: Centre
Height: 5'3" (1.61m)
Weight: 205lbs (93kg)
International Career: 1947 - 1951
International Caps: 23
International Points: 12
Honours: Five Nations Championship (1947, 1950), Five Nations Grand Slam (1950)

1980 Lions on their tour of South Africa as the team doctor.

He maintained a healthy interest in sport after retiring from rugby and became medical officer to the Welsh Boxing Association. He died aged 92 in 2012.

ABOVE Jack Matthews (right) touches down for a try

Meredith, Bryn

As probably the most powerful, technically gifted, sure-handed and mobile hooker in world rugby in the 1950s, South African pitches were made for Bryn Meredith. The Welshman thrived on his two Lions tours, playing in eight Tests and scoring a record six tries by a hooker.

Meredith played for Welsh Schools in 1949, Devonport Services, St Luke's College in the fabulous 1953 team, and appeared for Devon and South West Counties in their match against the touring New Zealanders later in the year. He also propped for Newport against the Kiwis as Lyn Davies had been drafted in at hooker.

He made such an impact on the tourists that the selectors gave Meredith his international debut for Wales in 1954. He secured the side so much clean ball from the scrum and lineout that Wales earned a share of the Five Nations title after wins over Ireland, France and Scotland. He then became a Lion the following season. Over the next eight years he missed only three games for his country and went on another two tours with the Lions. The tourists shared the 1955 series with the Springboks, with Meredith, along with fellow Welsh front-rowers Billy Williams and Courtney Meredith, the catalyst for an outstanding – albeit losing – performance in the second Test in Cape Town. They may have been smaller than their opposite numbers but they were more mobile around the park and technically superior at the set piece. Meredith's reputation was enhanced by winning crucial strikes and popping up in the backline to take the try-scoring pass from centre Phil Davies.

Wales narrowly missed out on a Grand Slam in 1955 after a six-point loss to Scotland – they shared the title with France – but they won the 1956 championship outright despite losing to Ireland. Meredith proved himself again on the 1959 Lions tour of Australia and New Zealand, although he had to compete with tour skipper Ronnie Dawson for a place in the Test team and only played in the provincial matches. He captained the side against the Junior All Blacks but this was scant consolation. He didn't complain, however, and even popped up as a flanker when injuries forced a reshuffle on the Australian leg of the tour.

In 1962, Meredith was thought to have a good chance of skippering the tourists in South Africa but he missed out to Arthur Smith. He cemented his reputation by being picked for all four Tests and disrupting the Springbok forwards with his all-action style. He retired at the end of the tour with eight Lions and 34 Welsh caps, and he was voted Welsh sportsman of the year in his final season.

Name: Brinley 'Bryn' Victor Meredith
Born: 21st October 1930, Abersychan, Wales
Position: Hooker
Height: 5'11" (1.80m)
Weight: 192lbs (87kg)
International Career: 1954 - 1962
International Caps: 42
International Points: 12
Honours: Lions Series Draw (1955), Five Nations Championship (1954, 1955, 1956)

BELOW Bryn Meredith (centre right) leaps high during a line-out

Meredith, Courtney

RIGHT Courtney Meredith

Meredith played for club side Neath before being called up for international duty with Wales. He was a powerful and technical prop who gave his pack a solid foundation and allowed them to win good set-piece ball. Having guided the side to the 1954 Five Nations title, he was selected for the Lions tour to South Africa the following year and was part of the all-Wales front row that included Billy Williams and namesake but no relation Bryn Meredith. The closely fought series ended 2-2.

His international career may have been relatively short – 14 appearances and one try in four years for Wales is unremarkable – but Meredith's contribution to the game is far greater. He was the cornerstone of a Lions pack that nullified the Springboks in the first and third Tests, and the tourists eventually won 19 of their 25 games. He was also instrumental in an international front row that won three consecutive Five Nations Championships.

Name: Courtney Charles Meredith
Born: 23rd September 1926, Pontypridd, Wales
Position: Prop
Height: 5'10" (1.78m)
Weight: 209lbs (95kg)
International Career: 1953 - 1957
International Caps: 17
International Points: 3
Honours: Lions Series Draw (1955), Five Nations Championship (1954, 1955, 1956)

Morgan, Clifford

Morgan was born into a mining family and he soon made an impact at Cardiff RFC in 1949. His natural flair saw him progress rapidly and by 1951 he'd made his international debut against his hero, Ireland's Jack Kyle. The following year he was the catalyst for Wales's backline moves and the side secured the Grand Slam. In 1953 he cemented his reputation as the greatest standoff in the game by guiding Cardiff and Wales to victory over the touring All Blacks.

If Tony O'Reilly was the star soloist for the 1955 Lions, Cliff Morgan was the conductor who called the tune. The South African media christened him 'Morgan the Magnificent' but the little Welshman had already earned his reputation as the finest standoff in the country. Now he was able to unleash one of the greatest Lions backlines, which included Jeff Butterfield, Arthur Smith, Cecil Pedlow and O'Reilly.

His blistering acceleration, a magical outside break and his elusive sidestep were his trademark, all of which were on show during the first Test, ranked by many as the greatest international ever played. The Lions were struggling after an injury to Reg Higgins reduced them to 14 men but Morgan broke from a scrum against the head and raced past Basie van Wyk to score the try that levelled the match. The world-record crowd of 100,000 knew they had witnessed something very special

His blistering acceleration, a magical outside break and his elusive sidestep were his trademark.

MORGAN, CLIFFORD

RIGHT Cliff Morgan

indeed and the Lions' 23-22 victory is still talked about today.

With captain Robin Thompson injured before the decisive third Test, the Lions turned to Morgan for inspiration. He roused the side pre-match with a stirring speech and then proceeded to pen the Springboks in their own half with a series of pinpoint kicks. Victory by nine points to six meant the Lions could not lose the rubber, but their hopes of outright victory were dealt a blow when Morgan turned an ankle before the final Test. He played through the pain but he was a shadow of the maestro in the previous match and the Lions couldn't prevent South Africa squaring the series. The Welshman's reputation as the finest standoff in the game was beyond doubt, however, and the South African press named him man of the series.

He returned home a national hero and was promptly given the national captaincy. He led Wales to the Five Nations title but they missed out on a Grand Slam after an eight-point defeat to Ireland in Dublin. England were the dominant force in the 1957 championship and secured their seventh Grand Slam, although Wales held them to a draw in 1958 and would have won the series had they not been beaten at home by the French in their last match.

Morgan retired from top-class rugby in 1958 with 33 international appearances behind him. He joined the BBC later in the year as a sports organiser for Wales, and he later became editor of *Sportsview* and *Grandstand*. He was also the editor of Sports Radio and head of outside broadcasts for radio and television until he retired in 1987. He also edited *Rugby: the Great Ones*, a list of the finest players that was published in 1970.

He was awarded an OBE in 1977, an

Name: Clifford Isaac Morgan, OBE
Born: 7th April 1930, Trebanog, Wales
Died: 29th August 2013
Position: Fly-half
Height: 5'7" (1.71m)
Weight: 156lbs (71kg)
International Career: 1951 - 1958
International Caps: 33
International Points: 12
Honours: Lions Series Draw (1955), Five Nations Championship (1952, 1954, 1955, 1956), Five Nations Grand Slam (1952)

honorary MA from the University of Wales in 1988, an honorary doctorate from Keele University in 1989, and was made a Fellow of the Polytechnic of Wales in 1989. He was also associated with several charities. His most famous moment in broadcasting came when he supplied the commentary to the greatest try in history, Gareth Edwards' score in the corner at Cardiff Arms Park after Phil Bennett had launched a risky counterattack for the Barbarians in their epic victory over the All Blacks in 1973.

Morgan was forced to retire from his broadcasting career when cancer of the vocal chords robbed him of the ability to speak. He was inducted into the IRB Hall of Fame in 2009 and retired to the Isle of Wight, but he died in 2013 at the age of 83.

The Welshman's reputation as the finest standoff in the game was beyond doubt.

Morgan, Teddy

Teddy Morgan's rugby career began at the relatively late age of 22. He'd qualified as a GP and moved from Sketty on the south coast of Wales to work at Guy's Hospital in London. He started playing with the Welsh exiles and earned selection to the national team in 1902 for their opening Home Nations Championship match against England at Blackheath. Wales won by a point and demolished Scotland three weeks later in Cardiff. They then thumped Ireland to complete a Triple Crown. (Winning all your matches against the other home unions wasn't known as a Grand Slam until 1957, by which time the French were part of the tournament. It was then applied retroactively to teams that had previously completed a clean sweep.)

Morgan was a key figure in the first golden age of Welsh rugby and he also took over the captaincy of the British Lions on their 1904 tour of Australia and New Zealand when Scotsman David Bedell-Sivright picked up an injury. He played in all four Tests and scored seven tries on the tour, touching down in the third match against Australia. Morgan was at the helm for the final three internationals, which included the first-ever Test between the Lions and All Blacks.

He then guided Wales to another Triple Crown the following year. He's perhaps best remembered for two contributions in the famous match against the 1905 All Blacks, however. In the middle of the first half, Dicky Owen released Cliff Pritchard who then fed Rhys Gabe. Gabe slipped the ball to Morgan and he dummied Kiwi fullback George Gillett before touching down in the corner for the decisive try. Later in the match, All Black centre Bobby Deans appeared to score for the tourists but he was tackled on the line by Pritchard and Gabe so the referee ruled that he'd landed just short.

MORGAN, TEDDY

Morgan said later that the grounding was in fact legal and the try should have stood.

Wales continued their dominance of the Home Nations Championship in 1906, although they shared the title with Ireland after losing in Belfast. A narrow loss to Scotland in 1907 denied Morgan another Triple Crown, but he was in the side that won the first ever Grand Slam the following year. Although their match against France didn't count towards the championship, Morgan ran in two tries and Wales won all four games convincingly. He retired at the end of the campaign and missed another Welsh Grand Slam in 1909.

A shooting accident in 1938 left him blinded in his right eye and he died at North Walsham in 1949 at the age of 69.

LEFT Teddy Morgan even made it onto a postcard in 1905

Name: Edward 'Teddy' Morgan
Born: 22nd May 1880, Aberdare, Wales
Died: 1st September 1949, North Walsham, England
Position: Wing
Height: 5'7" (1.71m)
Weight: 154lbs (70kg)
International Career: 1902 - 1908
International Caps: 20
International Points: 45
Honours: Five Nations Championship (1902, 1905, 1906, 1908), Five Nations Grand Slam (1908)

Morgan was a key figure in the first golden age of Welsh rugby and he also took over the captaincy of the British Lions on their 1904 tour of Australia and New Zealand.

Morris

Dai Morris was an old-school hard-man who worked shifts at the local pit before pulling on the red jersey. He'd served his apprenticeship with three local club sides before signing for Neath, and he was called up by the national team for the 1967 Five Nations. The side was in transition between the great team of the mid-1950s and the all-conquering class of the 1970s and a solitary win over England left them bottom of the championship. The 1968 campaign saw little improvement and Wales could only beat Scotland, but by 1969 the likes of Barry John and Gareth Edwards were coming into their prime. Wales were unbeaten and only an 8-8 draw with France in Paris denied them a Grand Slam.

RIGHT Dai Morris in his club colours

Morris wasn't shy about letting his team-mates know what he thought of their play and their behaviour off the field. Anything less than perfection in a match was unthinkable and losing concentration or not giving 100% was unacceptable. On a tour to New Zealand in 1970, some of the tougher players were misbehaving on a flight so Morris threatened to deck any of them who continued swaying the aircraft: everyone sat down.

His work ethic earned him the highest praise, however, and he only missed two Tests between his debut against France in 1967 and his final international against England at Twickenham seven years later. Gareth Edwards maintained that he never saw Morris put in anything but a full shift, and Barry John nicknamed him the 'Shadow' because he was always on his shoulder to take the killer pass. He was a key member of the Wales pack that won the Grand Slam in 1971 but he was inexplicably overlooked for the 1971 Lions tour to New Zealand. A brutal Tommy David tackle ruptured his cruciate ligaments and ended his career in 1974. Thirty years later, Morris was voted into the greatest-ever Welsh side as the blindside flanker.

Name: William David 'Dai' Morris
Born: 11th November 1941, Rhigos, Wales
Position: Flanker
Height: 6'0" (1.83m)
Weight: 175lbs (86kg)
International Career: 1967 - 1974
International Caps: 34
International Points: 19
Honours: Five Nations Championship (1969, 1970, 1971), Five Nations Grand Slam (1971)

BELOW The great Dai Morris

Nicholls

Nicholls joined Cardiff in 1893 and remained with the club for the next 18 seasons, with four of those as club captain. The first of his 24 international appearances came against Scotland in Cardiff in 1896, a match the hosts won by six. Having lost to England and Ireland, Wales finished bottom of the table.

The following year, Wales withdrew from the tournament after the Gould Affair – Arthur Gould had been offered money at his testimonial, which breached the rules on amateurism – so they only played one match, an 11-0 win over England.

The affair rumbled on into 1898 so it wasn't until the next season that Nicholls could light up pitches with his pace and running lines. He was selected for the 1899 tour to Australia on the back of an outstanding performance against England, in which Wales ran in six tries. He played in all four Tests for the British Isles and scored two tries.

He returned to the Welsh side for the Triple Crown seasons of 1900 and 1902, by which time he'd been named captain, and he was also at the helm for the historic win over the All Blacks in 1905. He scored a try and made another in Cardiff's heartbreaking 10-8 defeat to the tourists but he inspired them to a glorious 17-0 win over South Africa on New Year's Day in 1907. In all, Nicholls scored 111 tries in 242 games for Cardiff and captained them for four seasons. He also made 11 unbeaten appearances for Newport. Following his retirement after another successful Home Nations Championship in 1906, he officiated at the England-Scotland match during the 1909 tournament.

This prince of centres almost gave his own life while trying to rescue swimmers who had been caught in an undertow in Weston-super-Mare in 1923. He

RIGHT Gwyn Nicholls

Nicholls could light up pitches with his pace and running lines.

died in 1939 and was inducted into the International Rugby Hall of Fame in 2005. A pair of gates at Cardiff Arms Park were named in his honour on Boxing Day in 1949.

Name: Erith Gwyn Nicholls
Born: 15th July 1874, Westbury-on-Severn, England
Died: 24th March 1939, Powys, Wales
Position: Centre
International Career: 1896 - 1906
International Caps: 28
International Points: 19
Honours: Home Nations Championship (1900, 1902, 1905, 1906), Home Nations Triple Crown (1900, 1902, 1905), British Isles Series Winner (1899)

Norster

Bob Norster was an unsung hero in the Welsh pack during a torrid period in their history. His career began with Abertillery RFC before he moved to Cardiff and earned a call-up to the national team for the 1982 Five Nations. Wales beat France in Cardiff but lost their remaining games against the home unions and finished bottom of the table. Wales showed some improvement during the next campaign but a draw against England denied them a shot at the title.

Norster was selected for the Lions tour to New Zealand in 1983 but he only played two Tests and the hosts won the series 4-0, inflicting only the second whitewash on the Lions in a century. He returned for the 1984 Five Nations but Wales could only finish mid-table and it wasn't until the 1987 World Cup that the side finally found its feet. The Welsh topped their group and then beat England in the quarter-final in Brisbane but Norster was unavailable for the semi-final brawl against New Zealand and Wales eventually lost by 43 points.

Wales famously beat England again at Twickenham in 1988 and more wins over Scotland and Ireland saw the side host France in Cardiff with a Grand Slam up for grabs. Wales lost by a single point, however, and could only share the championship with Les Bleus. Norster toured with the Lions

He was then appointed manager of the national team and guided them to the 1994 Five Nations Championship.

RIGHT Bob Norster

...An unsung hero in the Welsh pack during a torrid period in their history.

in Australia in 1989 and helped the team to a series victory despite them losing the first Test. He retired from international rugby after playing for a World XV against South Africa in Johannesburg later that year.

He was then appointed manager of the national team and guided them to the 1994 Five Nations Championship.

Name: Robert Leonard 'Bob' Norster
Born: 23rd June 1957, Ebbw Vale, Wales
Position: Lock
Height: 6'5" (1.96m)
Weight: 232lbs (105kg)
International Career: 1982 - 1989
International Caps: 37
International Points: 8
Honours: World Cup Third Place (1987), Five Nations Championship (1988), Lions Series Winner (1989)

North

George North was raised on Angelsey but then went to Llandovery College on the mainland. He joined the Scarlets in 2010 and received an international call-up for the autumn series after only six matches. He scored two tries on his debut against reigning world champions South Africa, although Wales eventually lost a superb game 29-25. He missed most of the following Six Nations campaign and couldn't help Wales going down to a heavy defeat against France in their final match.

The World Cup in New Zealand allowed the giant wing to showcase his skills and many observers likened him to Jonah Lomu. Wales were narrowly beaten by defending champions South African in their opening match but they fought back to beat Samoa. He came on after an hour against Namibia and scored two tries and scored another against Fiji in a 66-0 rout. Wales eased past Ireland (22-10) in the quarter-final and would have made the final but for Warburton's sending off at Hook's two missed kicks in the semi against France.

North continued his good form with a try against Ireland in the opening match of the 2012 Six Nations but he came

Name: George Philip North
Born: 13th April 1992, King's Lynn, England
Position: Wing
Height: 6'4" (1.94m)
Weight: 240lbs (109kg)
International Career: 2010 - present
International Caps: 52
International Points: 120
Honours: Six Nations Championship (2012, 2013), Six Nations Grand Slam (2012), Lions Series Winner (2013)

RIGHT George North

off at half-time against Scotland. Wales won the match and then beat England the following week to keep their Grand Slam hopes alive. They then breezed past Italy and Halfpenny kicked them to victory over France to claim the title and the Grand Slam.

Wales began their defence poorly with an eight-point defeat to Ireland but North scored the only try of the match in a 10-point win over France in Paris. They again overcame Italy with ease and Halfpenny kicked them to victory over Scotland with 23 of his side's 28 points. The Welsh then denied England the Grand Slam and stole the championship with a 30-3 crushing of the old enemy in Cardiff.

North was named in the Lions squad to tour Australia later in the year and he scored a fabulous solo try after 25 minutes of the first Test in Brisbane. He almost added another a couple of minutes later but he brushed the touchline and it was disallowed. The Australian backs were thrown into disarray by injuries

ABOVE George North takes man and ball on the 2013 Lions tour of Australia

but Kurtley Beale still could have won the game for the hosts with two late penalties. He slipped while striking the second kick, however, gifting the Lions a two-point win. In the second Test, Australia scored the only try and Helfpenny's last-gasp kick fell short, setting up a decider in Sydney.

Sam Warburton and Paul O'Connell were both injured so Brian O'Driscoll was expected to skipper the side but Warren Gatland went with Jamie Roberts and Jonathan Davies in the centres. North scored his 14th Test try as the Lions demolished the Australians 41-16. He scored three more in the autumn series later that year and then another three in the 2014 Six Nations, although Wales slipped to mid-table after defeats to Ireland and England.

He was on sparkling form in the 2015 Six Nations and a hat-trick against Italy in Wales's last match would have given them the championship on points difference had Ireland and England not won their final matches convincingly.

Pask

Pask went to Loughborough University and played for Abertillery having graduated. A fantastic all-round athlete with a superb rugby brain, great handling skills and a ferocious tackle, he could have played in any era. He made his debut for Wales in 1961, scoring a try in the third match of the Five Nations against Ireland. Wales won the game and finished second in the championship after another victory over England. The following year he was selected to tour with the Lions and played in three of the four Tests against South Africa. Although the series wasn't a great success – the Lions lost three and drew one of the Tests – he was on the team-sheet for the next tour to Australia and New Zealand in 1966.

In the Five Nations before the tour, Pask was selected as captain and Wales duly lifted the trophy. They'd endured a barren period in the early part of the decade but by 1964 the national side was developing into the team that Edwards, John, Bennett and Davies would join before dominating northern hemisphere rugby for a generation. Wales built on the foundation of a solid forward pack and only missed out on a Grand Slam in 1965 when they lost the final game in Paris by nine points. They were then denied another Grand Slam by just three points in Dublin the following season.

The first part of the subsequent Lions tour was a great success and Pask played in both the wins over the Wallabies. He also played in three of the four unsuccessful games against the All Blacks,

His 22 games during the 1966 tour remains the record for the most number of games played for the Lions on a single trip

RIGHT Alun Edward Islwyn Pask

OPPOSITE Alun Pask (right) with teammates

the New Zealanders being in a different class. His 22 games during the 1966 tour remains the record for the most number of games played for the Lions on a single trip (he'd also made 16 appearances in South Africa for a total of 38 matchers for the Lions). He retired from international rugby the following year having racked up 26 appearances and two tries for Wales and eight Test starts for the Lions.

He died in 1995 at the age of only 58 after being overcome by smoke when he re-entered his burning house to rescue precious personal items.

Name: Alun Edward Islwyn Pask
Born: 10th September 1937, Blackwood, Wales
Died: 1st November 1995, Blackwood
Position: Flanker / Number 8
Height: 6'2" (1.88m)
Weight: 198lbs (90kg)
International Career: 1961 - 1967
International Caps: 34
International Points: 6
Honours: Five Nations Championship (1964, 1965)

Phillips

Mike Phillips was born into a sporting family – one brother was a national boxing champion and another played top-class rugby – and raised on a dairy farm. He was so tall that he started off as a flanker but his quick hands and breaks from the base of the scrum saw him sign for Scarlets as a scrum-half at the age of 20. He was Dwayne Peel's understudy so he eventually moved to Cardiff to give himself more game time.

He was called up to the national squad for a match against Romania in 2003 and he marked his debut with a try. Having missed out on selection for the World Cup, he toured Argentina, South Africa and North America. He was drafted into the squad for the Six Nations Grand Slam-winning side in 2005 but could only make the bench for the last two matches. He endured a torrid autumn series, which ended in a 41-3 defeat to the All Blacks, a narrow win over Fiji, a heavy loss to South Africa and another tight win against Australia.

The 2006 Six Nation was a disaster and Wales only managed a solitary win, but Phillips won the man-of-the-match award against France. He started both Tests against Argentina on the summer

Name: William Michael 'Mike' Phillips
Born: 29th August 1982, Carmarthen, Wales
Position: Scrum-half
Height: 6'3" (1.91m)
Weight: 223lbs (101kg)
International Career: 2003 - present
International Caps: 98
International Points: 50
Honours: Six Nations Championship (2008, 2012, 2013), Six Nations Grand Slam (2008, 2012), Lions Series Winner (2013)

RIGHT Mike Phillips

tour and began to make an impression on the national side but another dismal showing in the subsequent Six Nations halted his progress. The World Cup failure at the hands of Fiji in 2007 might have ended his career but Phillips forced his way back into Warren Gatland's team for the 2008 Six Nations and he scored the winning try against England. He was ever-present in the side that secured the Grand Slam with a thumping victory over the French but a knee ligament injury then sidelined him for six months. He also fell foul of the authorities after a number of disciplinary misdemeanours and had to fight to retain his place.

He toured with the 2009 Lions in South Africa and scored a try in the first Test. He also played in the crucial second Test but couldn't prevent the hosts taking an epic series. He finally usurped Dwayne Peel from the number-nine jersey and guided Wales to their third Grand Slam of the new millennium in 2012. He then toured with the Lions on their successful tour of Australia the following year and made the team for the first and decisive third Tests.

Price

Price was educated in Pontypool and was capped at schoolboy level. He then joined the local club as a tight-head prop after finishing his studies. (His career was inextricably linked with Pontypool and he wouldn't hang up his boots until playing his 600th game in 1992.) His power and technique brought him Welsh national athletics titles in the discus and shot and he also came to the attention of the national rugby selectors.

He collected his first Wales cap in 1975 alongside Pontypool stalwarts Bobby Windsor and Charlie Faulkner. He marked an astonishing debut by sprinting 70 metres to scoop up a loose ball and score after a French move had broken down in the Welsh 22. With six new caps in the side, Wales weren't expected to trouble the French but he helped demolish the opposing pack and their 25-10 victory silenced those who'd criticised his selection. Price was mighty relieved to have won over the doubters: "In some ways I'm glad that the try I scored on my debut for Wales came at the end of our game at Parc des Princes. Had it come at the beginning I'd have been physically and emotionally shattered for the rest of the match."

A two-point defeat to Scotland at Murrayfield denied them a Grand Slam but the Welsh side of the mid-1970s was virtually unplayable and they romped

He was proficient in the loose, and his handling and timing of the pass from contact allowed the speedsters to make use of the extra time and space he afforded them.

PRICE

LEFT Graham Price pictured during the Second Test match between New Zealand and the British Lions

to the title in 1976 with crushing wins over the other home unions and a six-point victory over France in Cardiff on the penultimate weekend of the championship.

A year later, the same three Pontypool men would dominate the Lions front row in tour matches against Counties, Bay of Plenty and Fiji. Price confirmed his status on the 1977 New Zealand tour as a prop of considerable ability in what was perhaps the strongest front five the game had yet seen. He withstood everything the All Blacks threw at him and was selected on the back of more good performances for Wales's tour of Australia the following year.

It was a brutal series that saw Price suffer a broken jaw when he was punched by Wallaby prop Steve 'The Gunfighter' Finnane during the second Test. Finnane claimed he threw the punch partly in self-defence and partly in retaliation for apparent Welsh brutality in the previous games. The front row had always been a dark and dirty place so both men had to shoulder some of the blame. Price recovered quickly, however, and was selected for his second Lions tour in 1980.

He fronted up to the huge Springbok pack in all four Tests and proved himself technically superior to the hosts, even scoring a try after a strong eight-man shove. He was also proficient in the loose, and his handling and timing of the pass from contact allowed the speedsters to make use of the extra time and space he afforded them.

By 1983 his career was winding down and, although selected for the tour to New Zealand, the Lions suffered a 4-0 series defeat. Price played in 12 successive matches for the Lions and he became the tourists' most-capped prop.

With the respect he deserved from the public, he retired from international rugby at the end of the tour. He racked up 41 caps for Wales and 12 for the Lions, both then records for a prop, with the latter unlikely to be broken now that tours are limited to three Tests.

Name: Graham Price, MBE
Born: 24th November 1951, Moascar, Egypt
Position: Prop
Height: 6'0" (1.83m)
Weight: 210lbs (95kg)
International Career: 1975 - 1983
International Caps: 53
International Points: 12
Honours: Five Nations Championship (1975, 1976, 1978, 1979), Five Nations Grand Slam (1976, 1978)

Quinnell, Derek

Quinnell was educated in Llanelli and joined his local club in 1967. He made such an impression that he was selected for the Lions tour to New Zealand in 1971 without having been capped by Wales. He made his debut under intense pressure in the cauldron of the third Test on the successful tour, but he had to wait until the following year before being capped by Wales (against France in the Five Nations).

ABOVE Derek Quinnell

He eventually won 23 caps for his country and was again selected for the Lions. He made two Test appearances in New Zealand in

He is one of very few players to have recorded four wins over the mighty All Blacks.

the epic 23-11 win at the Arms Park the following year.

All three of his sons played top-flight rugby, with Craig playing for Wales 32 times and scoring five tries, Scott being capped by his country (52 times with 11 tries) and by the Lions (three times with one try against Australia in 2001), and Gavin playing for the Scarlets until an eye injury ended his career. Derek went on to become a selector for both Wales and the Lions.

Name: Derek Leslie Quinnell
Born: 22nd May 1949, Llanelli, Wales
Position: Number 8
Height: 6'4" (1.92m)
Weight: 231lbs (105kg)
International Career: 1971 - 1980
International Caps: 28
International Points: 4
Honours: Five Nations Championship (1973, 1975, 1976, 1978, 1979), Five Nations Grand Slam (1976, 1978), Lions Series Winner (1974)

ABOVE Derek Quinnell in action

1977 and another two in South Africa three years later. He is one of very few players to have recorded four wins over the mighty All Blacks, two of which came with the Lions, one with Llanelli at their famous victory at Stradey Park in 1972, and then with the Barbarians in

Quinnell, Scott

One of the most powerful ball carriers to play for Wales, Quinnell captained his country seven times. The elder brother of fellow international Craig joined Llanelli juniors at the age of eight and made his senior debut in 1990 against Penygroes. He was selected for the national team in 1993 in a shock 26-24 home defeat to Canada but he scored a brilliant individual try against France in Cardiff as Wales won the Five Nations Championship the following spring.

He then switched codes to join rugby league giants Wigan for a world record £400,000. He spent two years with the side and also represented Wales at the 1995 Rugby League World Cup. When rugby union turned professional later that year, he switched back and joined Richmond. He was selected for the 1997 British & Irish Lions to South Africa but he didn't make the Test team as he had to return home for a double hernia operation.

He rejoined Llanelli the following year and was a huge presence in the Wales team that went on a 10-match winning streak under Graham Henry in 1999. Sadly the run came to an end at the hands of Samoa in their final pool match of the World Cup but Wales still reached the quarter-finals before going out to eventual winners Australia.

Quinnell scored 11 tries for Wales and was practically unstoppable from close-range. He also scored a brilliant solo effort as the Lions crushed Australia during the pulsating first

BELOW Quinnell breaches the Argentinian defence.

QUINNELL, SCOTT

Scott Quinnell celebrates a Welsh win

Test in Brisbane on the 2001 tour, but the Wallabies fought back to level the series in Melbourne and edged the decider in Sydney. He retired from international rugby at the end of the 2002 autumn internationals.

He helped Llanelli to the Welsh Cup and league title and was in the Scarlets side that lifted the Celtic League championship in 2004. He retired from all rugby at the end of the season to join Llanelli's coaching staff. Having guided the side to Welsh Cup glory, Quinnell stood down to concentrate on his work as pundit. He has also written newspaper columns and been chairman of the Welsh Rugby Players Association.

Name: Scott Quinnell
Born: 20th August 1972, Swansea, Wales
Position: Number 8
Height: 6'4" (1.93m)
Weight: 265lbs (120kg)
International Career: 1993 - 2002
International Caps: 55
International Points: 60
Honours: Five Nations Championship (1994), Lions Series Winner (1997)

Roberts

Jamie Roberts was born in Newport but he signed for Cardiff RFC in 2005 and racked up 28 appearances before joining the Blues. This brought him to the attention of the national selectors and he was drafted into the squad for the 2008 Six Nations after the side's disappointing showing at the previous year's World Cup.

He wasn't picked for the opener against England but he became the 1,057th player to pull on the red of Wales when he made his debut against Scotland at the Millennium Stadium in Cardiff the following week. Wales ran out 30-15 winners but Mark Jones took his place for the remainder of the Grand Slam-winning season. He scored his first try on the tough summer tour to South Africa but he was then moved into the centre for the autumn international series. In the epic final match against Australia, which Wales edged by three points, Roberts fractured his skull.

He returned for the 2009 Six Nations but was outplayed in the series decider by Brian O'Driscoll and Ireland claimed their first Grand Slam since 1948. The pair lined up together in midfield for the first Lions Test against South Africa but the tourists lost a pulsating game by five points. A last-minute Morné Steyn penalty in the second Test gave the hosts the series. Roberts sprained his wrist and missed the final Test, which the Lions won convincingly.

Roberts and James Hook's centre partnership developed throughout the 2010 Six Nations but the summer tour of South Africa and New Zealand was a disappointment and Roberts had surgery

Roberts is one of the most powerful ball carriers in world rugby

Jamie Roberts

on his wrist when he returned. Wales had a shot at the 2011 Six Nations title going into the final game against France but they were completely outplayed and eventually finished fourth.

The side finally blossomed at the 2011 World Cup and Roberts ran in two tries against Fiji. Wales made the semi-final after beating the Irish in the quarters but the French eked out a one-point win, and Wales then lost the third-place match to Australia. The Welsh continued to improve and dominated the 2012 Six Nations, claiming another Grand Slam after a 16-9 victory over France in their final game.

Name: Jamie Huw Roberts
Born: 8th November 1986, Newport, Wales
Position: Centre
Height: 6'4" (1.93m)
Weight: 242lbs (110kg)
International Career: 2008 - present
International Caps: 72
International Points: 50
Honours: Six Nations Championship (2008, 2012, 2013), Six Nations Grand Slam (2008, 2012), Lions Series Winner (2013)

Roberts was one of the standout players on the glorious 2013 Lions tour of Australia and he scored the final try of the decisive third Test in an overwhelming victory.

Roberts is one of the most powerful ball carriers in world rugby

Wales then inexplicably slumped to defeat in all four autumn internationals but recovered from a loss against Ireland in the first match of the subsequent Six Nations to take the overall title. Roberts was one of the standout players on the glorious 2013 Lions tour of Australia and he scored the final try of the decisive third Test in an overwhelming victory.

He then helped Wales to three wins in the 2014 Six Nations and another two, including a memorable victory over South Africa, in the autumn internationals. Wales would have won a Grand Slam in 2015 had they not lost narrowly to England. Instead, they eventually finished third in the Six Nations Championship.

Squire

Although he was an extremely useful cricketer, Squire captained St Luke's at rugby before moving to Cross Keys RFC. He served his apprenticeship with Newbridge, Newport (where he won the Welsh Cup) and Pontypool before being called up to the national squad in 1977. He played in two matches of that year's Five Nations campaign and made enough of an impact to be selected for the Lions tour to New Zealand later that year.

BELOW Jeff Squire releases the ball from a maul

It proved to be a tough series but he featured in a couple of the Tests. His form with Wales was outstanding the following year and he helped them to a Grand Slam with emphatic victories over the home unions and France. In 1980 he toured South Africa but the Lions were again outplayed, as indeed they were back in New Zealand in 1983. Professionalism had been

...His form with Wales was outstanding the following year and he helped them to a Grand Slam.

creeping into southern hemisphere rugby and the north simply couldn't cope with the power and pace of the All Blacks.

Squire was on the board of Welsh selectors from 1988 until 1990 but he stepped down when coach John Ryan resigned following a humiliating 34-6 defeat against England at Twickenham.

Name: Jeffrey Squire
Born: 23rd September 1951, Pontywaun, Wales
Position: Flanker / Number 8
Height: 6'3" (1.91m)
Weight: 214lbs (97kg)
International Career: 1977 - 1983
International Caps: 35
International Points: 12
Honours: Five Nations Championship (1978, 1979), Five Nations Grand Slam (1978)

Jeff Squire

Taylor

Taylor was born in Watford and played for London Welsh. He won his first cap for Wales in 1967 at the age of 21 and then played 26 Tests during the golden era of Welsh rugby in the 1970s. His greatest moment for his country came during a Five Nations game against Scotland at Murrayfield in 1971.

The balance of the match had shifted several times but the scores were still close in the dying minutes. With only seconds to go, it was 18-14 to the hosts when Wales earned a lineout on the Scotland 22-metre line. The Welsh won the ball and passed it along the three-quarters to winger Gerald Davies, who managed to squeeze in at the right-hand corner to score a remarkable try. Wales were still a point behind, however, and the conversion from the touchline looked almost impossible. Barry John would normally have taken the kick but he had been concussed earlier in the match so the left-footed Taylor stepped up and knocked over an extraordinary kick, described by one journalist as the 'greatest conversion since St Paul'. It was a pivotal moment in the championship as the one-point win gave Wales the confidence to secure

Name: John Taylor
Born: 21st July 1945, Watford, England
Position: Flanker
Height: 5'11" (1.80m)
Weight: 189lbs (86kg)
International Career: 1967 - 1973
International Caps: 30
International Points: 25
Honours: Five Nations Championship (1969, 1970, 1971, 1973), Five Nations Grand Slam (1971), Lions Series Winner (1971)

LEFT John Taylor in action

a historic Grand Slam with victory over France in Paris.

Taylor toured with the Lions in 1968 and again in 1971, although he played no Tests on his first tour. In the second, he played in all four Tests and helped the Lions beat the All Blacks for the only time in the tourists' history. He refused to tour South Africa in the apartheid era and wouldn't even play the Springboks when they visited the UK in 1969-70.

He retired in 1978 and began a successful career in broadcasting and journalism, notably with ITV where he was the lead at several World Cups and also called England's dramatic 2003 win over Australia in the final. He's now a regular behind the microphone for talkSport radio.

...Taylor stepped up and knocked over an extraordinary kick, described by one journalist as the 'greatest conversion since St Paul'.

Thomas

It was a controversial decision to select uncapped Welsh lock Delme Thomas for the 1966 Lions tour to New Zealand when there were several internationally accomplished rivals in the mix. When the tourists returned, however, his inclusion was viewed as one of the management's few good decisions. He would go on to play an astonishing 44 Test and provincial games for the tourists between 1966 and 1971.

Thomas first played against the All Blacks on their tour of the British Isles in 1963. He'd been impressed with their physicality and dominance at the set piece so he bulked up and improved his lineout skills. Three years later, he was deputising for the incomparable Rhys Williams at Stradey Park, Llanelli, and he immediately justified his selection on the tour to New Zealand by taking tour captain Mike Campbell-Lamerton's place for the second Test. With the captain reinstated for the third match, the management found room for Thomas at prop, an unprecedented move that only enhanced his reputation within the squad.

He again played in the front row on the 1968 tour to South Africa, although by now he was firmly established in the Welsh side. He twice faced up

Name: Delme Thomas
Born: 12th September 1942, Carmarthen, Wales
Position: Lock / Prop
Height: 6'2" (1.88m)
Weight: 222lbs (101kg)
International Career: 1966 - 1974
International Caps: 32
International Points: 0
Honours: Five Nations Championship (1969, 1970, 1971, 1973) Five Nations Grand Slam (1971)

RIGHT Another lineout to the British Lions as Delme Thomas (right) climbs above New South Wales's Owen Butler

...The management found room for Thomas at prop, an unprecedented move that only enhanced his reputation within the squad.

to the mighty Springbok forwards, coming on as a replacement in the third Test and starting the fourth. He still hadn't been on the winning side but the team was in transition and only reaped the rewards on the 1971 tour to New Zealand. He was again in the midst of the action, appearing in three of the four Tests and playing an important role in the series-opening win. He eventually played in 14 of the 24 tour matches before returning and winning the last of his 25 caps with Wales (he also captained the side once against New Zealand in 1972).

He retired from international rugby in 1974 having also guided Llanelli to their historic 9-3 win over the All Blacks and being a member of the immortal 1971 Welsh Grand Slam side.

Warburton

Warburton has English parents but he was born in Wales and chose to play in the red jersey rather than the white. He initially showed promise as a footballer, however, and played alongside Gareth Bale in his youth. He devoted his life to rugby in his teens and enjoyed three seasons with Glamorgan Wanderers before joining Cardiff Blues in 2009.

Warburton captained the Welsh Under-18s and then led the Under-19s and Under-20s to the semi-finals of the World Cup. He continued his meteoric rise by playing for the full international side against the USA in 2009. He was drafted into the squad for the 2010 Six Nations but had to wait a year for his first try against Italy the following season. Wales were a side in transition, however, and they didn't realize their potential until the 2011 World Cup, by which time Warburton had been appointed as captain (the second youngest after Gareth Edwards).

The open-side flanker was outstanding in Wales's opening match against South Africa. The defending champions were constantly pushed back by his tackling and endless work-rate at the breakdown. Although Wales lost a gripping match by a point, Warburton put in a man-of-the-match performance. He then guided the side through tricky encounters with Samoa and Ireland in the quarter-final.

His World Cup came to a controversial conclusion when he was sent off by Alain Rolland for a dangerous tackle on Vincent Clerc in the semi-final against France. Warburton admitted the offence but impartial observers thought Rolland's decision extremely harsh and a yellow card would have sufficed. The French still struggled to overcome 14-man Wales but they eventually won 9-8.

RIGHT Sam Warburton

The 2012 Six Nations campaign saw Warburton retained as captain and, although injury kept him out of two games, he led the side to a historic Grand Slam. He was at the helm for the 2013 Six Nations, which saw Wales lose their opening match to Ireland but win their remaining games to retain the title, and was then appointed captain of the 2013 Lions tour to Australia. He put in two of the great Lions performances and, despite being ruled out of the decisive third Test with a hamstring injury, led the side to the coveted series win.

Name: Sam Kennedy-Warburton
Born: 5th October 1988, Cardiff, Wales
Position: Flanker
Height: 6'2" (1.88m)
Weight: 234lbs (106kg)
International Career: 2009 - present
International Caps: 55
International Points: 20
Honours: Six Nations Championship (2012, 2013), Six Nations Grand Slam (2012), Lions Series Winner (2013)

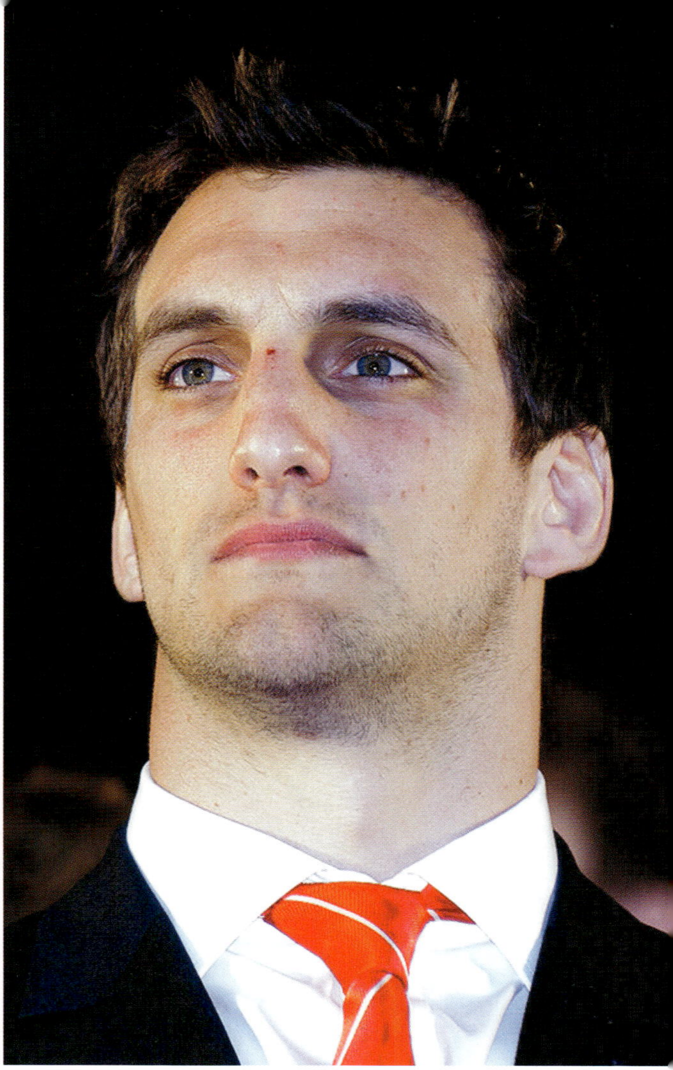

Warburton lines up the English attack

Williams, Bleddyn

When Lions' captain Karl Mullen was injured on the eve of the third Test against New Zealand in 1950, the tourists turned to Bleddyn Williams as his replacement. He was already Mullen's vice-captain and had been given the job of out-thinking the hosts tactically. He was perhaps the most complete centre of his generation and the flair player in the midfield.

Williams went to Rydal School in Colwyn Bay at the age of 14 after being recommended for a scholarship by cricket and rugby legend Wilf Wooller, a past pupil who inspired the Welsh to beat the 1935 All Blacks. He left school at 18 but his sporting career was cut short by the Second World War, during which he trained as a fighter pilot in Arizona. He switched to gliders after D-Day and crash-landed near the Rhine with a cargo of medical supplies. He spent a week sleeping in ditches before bumping into his commanding officer, Hugh Bartlett, one of the most famous cricketers in the country. Upon finding Williams, Bartlett is said to have exclaimed: "Aren't you supposed to be playing at Welford Road tomorrow for Great Britain against the Dominions? They need you. Go now!" Williams caught a plane to RAF Brize Norton that night and scored a wonderful try in a losing cause the next afternoon.

His raw talent was soon spotted by Cardiff and he was called up to the national team in 1947. Wales won the Five Nations Championship five times during his nine-year career, and in 1950 and 1952 secured Grand Slams. He was captain for five games in this glorious period for Welsh rugby and led the side to victory every time.

Every centre needs the right attributes and the Welshman was blessed with quick and accurate hands, a sidestep off both feet, solid defence, and great positional awareness, which he later shared as a respected rugby correspondent. Williams's skills had already brought him to the attention of Cardiff and Wales when the Lions came calling. He teamed up with club-mate Jack Matthews and the pairing proved irresistible on the 1950 tour to New Zealand and Australia.

He was injured for the first Test but he recovered and played 20 of the team's 29 matches, scoring 13 tries, including one in the victory over Australia in the first Test. He then captained the Lions in the third and fourth Tests in New Zealand, although the tourists came up just short in both, particularly the decisive final match in which Williams was denied the winning score by Peter Henderson.

He did finally beat the All Blacks with both Cardiff (8-3) and Wales (13-8) at the Arms Park in 1953. Both matches were played within a month and this was the national team's last victory over the All Blacks. With professional rugby in Wales having gone regional and touring teams usually only playing internationals, this remarkable feat is unlikely to be equalled. He retired in 1955 with 27 international caps and 24 points to his name, a rugby legend for club, country and the Lions.

After retiring, Bleddyn was appointed rugby correspondent for the Sunday People and was Welsh marketing manager for Wimpey Construction. His book Rugger, My Life was published the following year. He collapsed with an embolism at his Cardigan holiday home in 1995 but his wife revived him and he made a remarkable recovery. He died after a short illness in 2009.

Name: Bleddyn Williams, MBE
Born: 22nd February 1923, Taff's Well, Wales
Died: 6th July 2009, Cardiff
Position: Centre
Height: 5'10" (1.78m)
Weight: 182lbs / (83kg)
International Career: 1947 - 1955
International Caps: 27
International Points: 24
Honours: Five Nations Championship (1947, 1950, 1952, 1954, 1955), Five Nations Grand Slam (1950, 1952), Lions Series Winner (1950)

LEFT Bleddyn Williams delivers a pass for Cardiff Blues

Williams, JJ

The Lions tours of 1974 and 1977 highlighted the northern hemisphere's technique and forward power and they also introduced the south to one of the sport's great finishers, Welsh wing JJ Williams. He had represented his country in the short sprints at the 1970 Commonwealth Games but, by 1974, he was focusing on rugby. (JJ had also been British Schools 100m and 200m athletics champion and had competed for the United Kingdom at the World Student Games in Turin.) Having joined Bridgend, he scored 100 tries in 99 matches before moving to Llanelli and helping the side to the seminal victory over the All Blacks at Stradey Park in 1972.

In only his second top-flight season the 26-year-old schoolteacher took unpaid leave to tour South Africa with the 1974 Lions, but his 12 tries from as many games and four in the Test series immediately brought him to the attention of planet rugby. Pace may have been his primary weapon but speed alone is not enough when up against the best cover and rush defences. He soon developed a delicate kick and chase, slick hands, and a penchant for attacking the blindside with scrum-half Gareth Edwards. Against a South West Districts XV, he equalled David Duckham's record of six tries in a game. He scored again in the second and third Tests to help seal the series win.

Three years later, Williams toured New Zealand, although his trip was curtailed by a hamstring injury in the third Test. By then he'd already scored 10 tries, however, this despite poor weather and dreadful pitches nullifying his trademark chip and chase. He was again on hand to touch down in the second Test after a brilliant dummy.

He retired from international rugby in 1979 with 30 consecutive interna-

RIGHT John J Williams

Pace may have been his primary weapon but speed alone is not enough... He soon developed a delicate kick and chase, slick hands, and a penchant for attacking the blindside.

tionals for Wales, four Triple Crowns, two Grand Slams and four outright Five Nations titles. He is also the only Welsh player to have scored a hat-trick against Australia, which came in 1975 at Cardiff Arms Park. He became a straight-talking pundit with BBC Wales and now runs a commercial painting company. All three of his children have competed internationally in athletics and rugby.

Name: John James 'JJ' Williams, MBE
Born: 1st April 1948, Maesteg, Wales
Position: Wing
Height: 5'9" (1.75m)
Weight: 163lbs (74kg)
International Career: 1973 - 1979
International Caps: 37
International Points: 68
Honours: Five Nations Championship (1973, 1975, 1976, 1978, 1979), Five Nations Grand Slam (1976, 1978), Lions Series Winner (1974)

Williams, JPR

The attacking fullback role may have been developed by Ken Scotland in the 1950s, but it was JPR who turned it into an art form during the early 1970s. Williams was a superb all-round sportsman who won junior tennis and squash tournaments in 1966. He decided to concentrate on rugby, however, and moved to London Welsh in 1968. He made his debut for Wales on his 20th birthday the following year and made such an impression that he was selected for the Lions in 1971, where he proved himself the tourists' best number 15.

Fearless in the tackle, secure under the high ball, and devastating in attack, JPR also had a precision kicking game (in attack and defence) and he was particularly effective when exploiting the opposition's tactical inadequacies. In fact every kick he returned seemed to go back with interest, but he knew keeping the ball in play was more important than looking for touch because it kept the attacking options open. He hit the line with such pace that the opposition was immediately on the back foot, and the timing of his passes and his general creativity split unprepared defences.

Williams never shirked physical confrontation and in 1974 he had to be restrained by the police when tangling with Springbok great Tommy Bedford.

For Wales he was quite simply incomparable: he won an astonishing six outright Five Nations titles, six Triple Crowns and three Grand Slams.

JPR Williams, one of rugby's legends, in action

In all, he made 30 appearances for the Lions, including eight Test matches. He scored 16 points in 1971 and 12 in 1974, which included five tries. And he sealed the 1971 series with a rare 50-yard drop goal in the fourth Test.

For Wales he was quite simply incomparable: he won an astonishing six outright Five Nations titles, six Triple Crowns and three Grand Slams as Wales dominated the magical 1970s. JPR may have forged a reputation with his counterattacking and kicking but he was a formidable tackler too. His shoulder charge on Jean Francois Gourdon in 1976 prevented a try and nearly dumped the French wing into the crowd at Cardiff Arms Park as Wales secured another Grand Slam.

Fearless in the tackle, secure under the high ball, and devastating in attack, JPR also had a precision kicking game.

He finally retired in 1981 with 55 Welsh caps and 36 points under his belt. He was never on the losing side against England and guided the glorious national team alongside Gareth Edwards. He chose to continue his career as an orthopaedic surgeon rather than join the 1977 Lions in New Zealand but he carried on playing at domestic level with Tondu and didn't retire from club rugby until 2003. Arguably the best fullback of all time, JPR is now an ambassador for the sport, a true Welsh rugby legend.

Name: John Peter Rhys 'JPR' Williams, MBE
Born: 2nd March 1949, Cardiff, Wales
Position: Fullback
Height: 6'1" (1.85m)
Weight: 190lbs (86kg)
International Career: 1969 - 1981
International Caps: 63
International Points: 39
Honours: Five Nations Championship (1969, 1970, 1971, 1973, 1975, 1976, 1978, 1979), Five Nations Grand Slam (1971, 1976, 1978), Lions Series Winner (1971, 1974)

LEFT JPR Williams kicks under pressure from the South African defence

Williams, Martyn

Williams was a member of the successful Welsh Schools, Youth and Under-19 sides, and he also turned out for Wales A. His tireless work-rate in the back row brought him to the attention of the national selectors and he made his debut against the Barbarians in 1996. This was a lean period for Welsh rugby, however, and despite a brief resurgence under Graham Henry, it wasn't until Steve Hansen took over in 2002 that Wales finally emerged from the international wilderness. Williams, so often a bit-part player, was now at the forefront of Hansen's masterplan.

Williams played in the 2003 and 2007 World Cups and captained Wales on five occasions but he wasn't a successful skipper and was overlooked for leadership duties in 2003, a tournament lit up by the side's attacking philosophy. The flanker was then instrumental in the 2005 and 2008 Grand Slam seasons. He was voted the man of the tournament in 2005 after his two tries in Paris galvanised the Welsh and saw them make an unlikely comeback. He also scored another crucial try against the French to secure his second Grand Slam.

He won Welsh Cup and League honours with Pontypridd, the cup with

Name: Martyn Elwyn Williams, MBE
Born: 1st September 1975, Pontypridd, Wales
Position: Flanker
Height: 6'1" (1.85m)
Weight: 214lbs (97kg)
International Career: 1996 - 2012
International Caps: 104
International Points: 73
Honours: Six Nations Championship (2005, 2008, 2012), Six Nations Grand Slam (2005, 2008, 2012)

...The flanker was then instrumental in the 2005 and 2008 Grand Slam seasons. He was voted the man of the tournament in 2005 after his two tries in Paris.

Cardiff and was captain of the Cardiff Blues regional team. Williams was also a British & Irish Lion in Australia (2001) and New Zealand (2005). He came on as a replacement at the end of the final Test against the All Blacks, although the series had already been lost.

He was also selected for the 2009 Lions in South Africa. He came on late in the first two Tests but couldn't prevent the world champions edging the tourists in both games and winning the series. He retired shortly after earning his 100th cap in 2012.

LEFT Martyn Williams crashes over for a try

Williams, Rhys

Williams was educated at Ystalyfera Grammar School and Cardiff University, where he gained a reputation as a fine second-row forward. He made his debut for Llanelli aged 19 and went on to captain the side in the late 1950s. He also played for the RAF having qualified as an education officer.

He collected his first Wales cap against Ireland in the 1954 Five Nations, and he was also selected to tour with the Lions to South Africa the following year. It was a successful trip and the Lions shared the Test series against a strong Springbok outfit. Four years later, Williams toured again, this time to Australia and New Zealand. In the final Test of the Australian leg of the tour he took six consecutive lineouts to deny the hosts a chance of squaring the match, and he was then voted player of the series.

In all he played in 10 consecutive Tests for the tourists, winning two against South Africa, two against Australia and one against the All Blacks, and it was the Kiwis who paid him perhaps the greatest tribute after the Lions had won the

RIGHT Rhys Williams (centre, rear) during a team photo shoot

...He'd made such an impression, however, that he was invited to the All Blacks' private post-match function and was presented with an All Black jersey. No greater mark of respect could be asked, no greater compliment paid.

final test in Auckland. Williams had played in all four games but the first three had been won convincingly by the hosts. He'd made such an impression, however, that he was invited to the All Blacks' private post-match function and was presented with an All Black jersey. No greater mark of respect could be asked, no greater compliment paid. His presence in the scrum, power in the loose and ability to win vital ball at the restart and lineout sees Williams repeatedly voted into the all-time Welsh team.

Name: Rhys Haydn Williams
Born: 14th July 1930, Cwmllynfell, Wales
Died: 27th January 1993, Whitchurch, England
Position: Lock
Height: 6'3" (1.91m)
Weight: 234lbs (106kg)
International Career: 1954 - 1960
International Caps: 33
International Points: 0
Honours: Five Nations Championship (1954, 1955, 1956), Lions Series Draw (1955)

Williams, Shane

Shane Williams was one of the most devastating finishers in the game. Slight of build but nimble of foot and with electrifying pace over short distances, he left even the best defences clutching thin air.

His size led some to doubt him in his early career, and a spate of injuries threatened to derail his ascent to greatness, but he made his debut in 2000. More injury problems and general apathy from the Welsh coaching panel saw him sidelined until 2003 but he returned in time to claim a place at that year's World Cup. He lit up the tournament and finally silenced his critics with his lightning breaks, competence under the high ball and several huge performances, notably against New Zealand and England, albeit in losing causes.

Williams scored the crucial try against England and was omnipresent in the Grand Slam-winning Welsh side of 2005. This earned him a call-up to the Lions squad, but he only played in one Test in New Zealand and the tourists were soundly beaten. He was back to his brilliant best during the 2007 World Cup when he scored six tries, including a magnificent solo effort against Fiji. After another Grand Slam the following season, he was voted IRB Player of the Year and the Lions

RIGHT Shane Williams breaks away

...He lit up the tournament and finally silenced his critics with his lightning breaks, competence under the high ball and several huge performances.

came calling again in 2009. He was underused due to a slight dip in form but he still scored twice in the Lions' consolation victory.

Injury ruled him out of the 2011 Six Nations but Williams returned for the World Cup and helped Wales to fourth place in what was a magnificent tournament. He made his final Test appearance against Australia in December 2011, capping an outstanding international career with a try.

Williams will be remembered as one of the best wingers in world rugby. His flat speed, wicked sidestep and eye for a gap endeared him to fans and more than compensated for

Name: Shane Mark Williams, MBE
Born: 26th February 1977, Swansea, Wales
Position: Wing
Height: 5'7" (1.70m)
Weight: 176lbs (80kg)
International Career: 2000 - 2013
International Caps: 91
International Points: 300
Honours: Six Nations Championship (2005, 2008, 2012), Six Nations Grand Slam (2005, 2008, 2012)

his slightly shaky defence. Attacking rugby had been the hallmark of all the great Welsh teams and Williams brought his flair and excitement to a new generation. He bowed out with 91 international appearances and 60 tries to his name, placing him third on the all-time list. He retired in 2012 to take up a backroom role with the Ospreys and was scheduled to commentate on the 2013 Lions tour to Australia when he was unexpectedly called up to the squad for the match against the ACT Brumbies.

Shane Williams celebrates after scoring a try during the RBS Six Nations Championship match between Wales and France

Windsor

Willie John McBride may have had his hand on the tiller during the Lions tour to South Africa in 1974, but few of his foot soldiers encapsulated the winning mentality more than hooker Bobby Windsor. The Pontypool steelworker brought a mix of technical excellence, raw courage and outright aggression that lifted the entire squad on their way to series victory.

'The Duke', as his team-mates liked to call the former outside-half, was taught by the great coach Ray Prosser, but he was still a somewhat surprising choice to join the Lions given that he'd only just started playing for Wales. Whether he listened to the doubters or not is unknown but he knuckled down and forced his way into the Test side ahead of Ken Kennedy.

Windsor was one of the characters of the touring party and was soon selling excess kit to raise cash. On the pitch he was combative and courageous in the face of the big Springbok forwards, but he was also an asset in the loose with his quick hands and hard tackling. With Fran Cotton and Ian McLauchlan on either side, the trio of pocket-battleships sank the Springbok pack.

By 1977, Windsor was playing in a front row for Pontypool and Wales

On the pitch he was combative and courageous in the face of the big Springbok forwards, but he was also an asset in the loose with his quick hands and hard tackling.

RIGHT Bobby Windsor (centre) about to hit the scrum machine

that included Charlie Faulkner and Graham Price. This new forward line, known as the 'Viet-Gwent', travelled to New Zealand and dominated the provincial sides, although, possibly to the side's detriment, they were not given the Test berths and the series was lost. Price played in all four internationals but Faulkner was kept out by Cotton, and Windsor was controversially dropped after the first Test for Peter Wheeler.

Windsor played at the end of a golden era for Welsh rugby. He racked up 28 consecutive caps and helped the side win five Five Nations Championships, four Triple Crowns and two Grand Slams. Thereafter, Welsh fortunes declined and they wouldn't win another until 2005.

Windsor retired from international rugby in 1979 and finally published his autobiography, *The Iron Duke*, in 2010.

Name: Robert William 'Bobby' Windsor
Born: 31st January 1948, Newport, Wales
Position: Hooker
Height: 5'9" (1.75m)
Weight: 205lbs (93kg)
International Career: 1973 - 1979
International Caps: 33
International Points: 4
Honours: Five Nations Championship (1973, 1975, 1976, 1978, 1979), Five Nations Grand Slam (1976, 1978), Lions Series Winner (1974)

Young

Young was a mobile but combative prop who would eventually play both rugby codes at the highest level for more than 18 years. He was called up by Wales during the 1987 Rugby World Cup when Stuart Evans was ruled out with a broken foot (he happened to be playing his club rugby in Australia and was able to join the team immediately). He made a sensational debut in the 16-3 quarter-final win over England in Brisbane and he retained his place for the record 49-6 defeat by eventual world champions New Zealand in the semi-final. The match was a brutal encounter and he missed the third-place play-off victory over Australia.

He became a permanent fixture in the front row the following season as Wales won a Triple Crown for the first time in nine years. He also played in both Tests on Wales's summer 'tour of death' to New Zealand in 1988. The trip was so poorly organised and the schedule so brutal that several of the top players defected to rugby league, something which he considered but didn't act upon for another year.

He played in all three Tests for the Lions against Australia in 1989, and it was his abrasive approach upfront that helped starve the Wallabies of quick ball. When he returned to the UK he was snapped up by Leeds rugby league in a lucrative deal but he soon switched to Salford. He captained Wales in the 13-man code at the 1995 World Cup before returning to union in 1996. The following year he was again chosen to join the Lions in South Africa, although he didn't make the Test side. He toured with the team for a third time in Australia in 2001 but he was again a midweek player rather than a Test candidate.

Having rejoined domestic side Cardiff, he led the side for four seasons and became the 113th captain of Wales when he succeeded Rob Howley in 2000. He had already succeeded Graham Price as Wales's most-capped prop when he made his 42nd appearance but a recurring calf injury interrupted his career and could only be cured with an operation. He resigned as Wales captain and retired from international rugby following two humiliating defeats, a record 36-6 loss to Ireland at the Millennium Stadium in 2006 and a 30-16 home loss to Argentina that saw his leadership come in for widespread criticism. Wales won six of their 12 Tests with Young at the helm but he retired from international rugby in 2002 after racking up 51 union and 14 league caps.

His club career was far from over, however. He joined Cardiff Blues in 2003 and coached the side to a Heineken Cup semi-final and the Anglo-Welsh title in 2009. He was also at the tiller when the Blues became the first Welsh provincial side to claim a European title. In 2011, Young left the Blues and took over as Director of Rugby with Premiership heavyweights London Wasps.

Name: David 'Dai' Young
Born: 26th July 1967, Aberdare, Wales
Position: Prop
Height: 6'2" (1.88m)
Weight: 259lbs (117kg)
International Career: 1987 - 2001
International Caps: 54
International Points: 4
Honours: World Cup Third Place (1987), Five Nations Championship (1988), Lions Series Winner (1989)

ABOVE David 'Dai' Young was a giant in both rugby codes

All images in this book are copyright and have been provided courtesy of the following:

WIKICOMMONS
commons.wikimedia.org

GETTY IMAGES
101 Bayham Street, London NW1 0AG

Design & Artwork: ALEX YOUNG

Published by: DEMAND MEDIA LIMITED

Publisher: JASON FENWICK

Written by: LIAM McCANN